“From the beginning we h
and Womanhood that the
the authority and sufficiency of Scripture. Here you will find answers to key questions in a concise format from two of the evangelical community’s finest minds. May God use this book to encourage heartfelt obedience to his good and wise design.”

Randy Stinson, Provost and Senior Vice President for Academic Administration, The Southern Baptist Theological Seminary

“To borrow a phrase from C. S. Lewis, there’s a kind of ‘Deep Magic’ about the way God created man and woman—an ancient wonder that few of us postmoderns appreciate. Through a pragmatic arrangement of *50 Crucial Questions*, Piper and Grudem bring out passage after passage of Scripture to awaken our minds and hearts to the wonder of what our Creator has done. This concise treatment of the major questions surrounding our roles in the church and home will catapult readers straight into God’s Word to see what is really there.”

Gloria Furman, pastor’s wife, Redeemer Church of Dubai; author, *The Pastor’s Wife* and *Missional Motherhood*

“The core content of this book was tremendously needed and helpful when it was first published almost a quarter century ago. In our current generation, where there is breathtaking confusion and distortion regarding gender and marriage, it is needed more than ever. There is a desperate need for leaders of the evangelical church to speak with a wise, clear, and uncompromising biblical clarity. Piper and Grudem provide that clear voice, and I pray their answers will be heard and practiced so that God’s glory will be more powerfully displayed through his grand design for men and women.”

Erik Thoennes, Professor of Biblical and Theological Studies, Chair, Biblical and Theological Studies Theology Department, Talbot School of Theology, Biola University; Pastor, Grace Evangelical Free Church, La Mirada, California

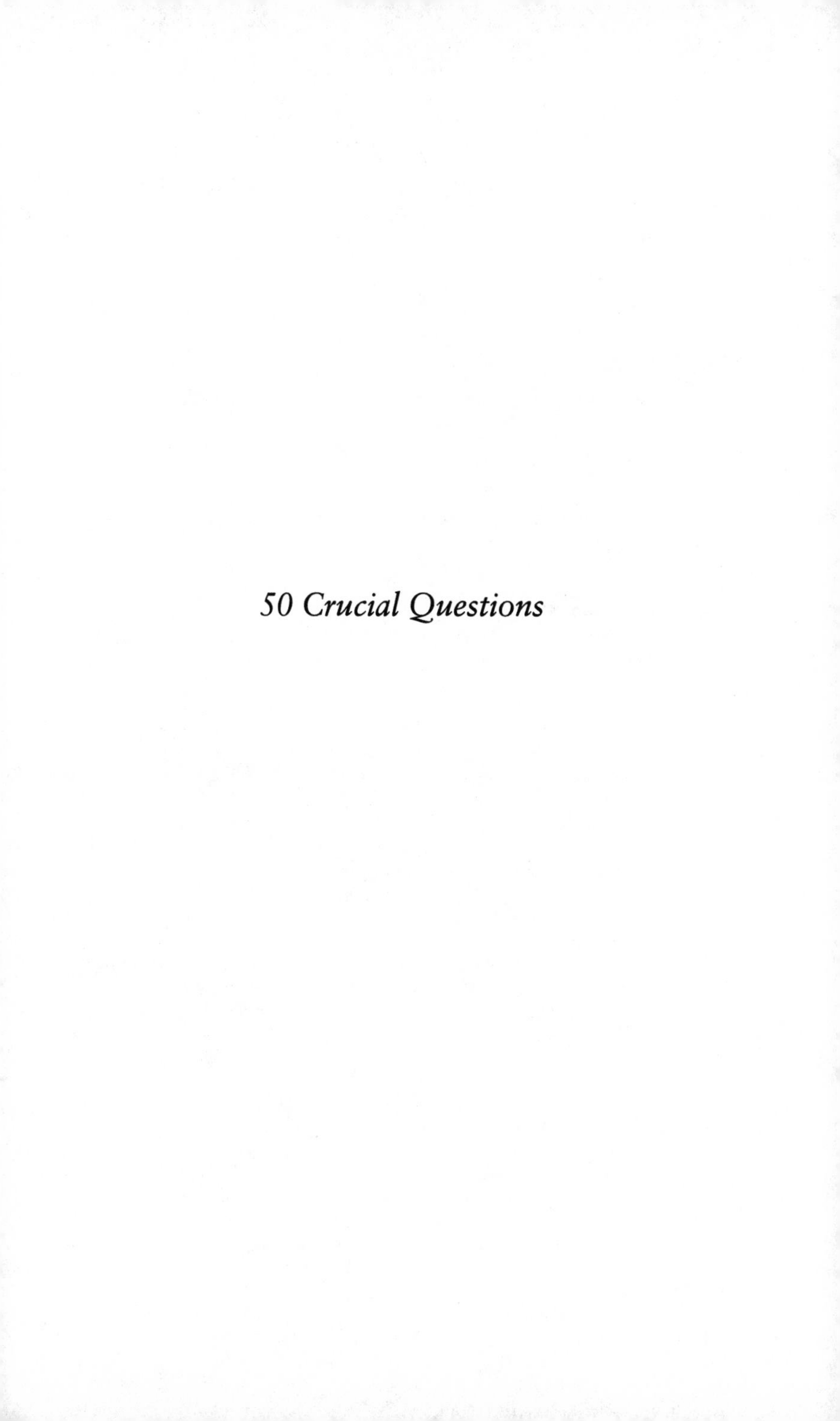

50 Crucial Questions

50 Crucial Questions

An Overview of Central Concerns about Manhood and Womanhood

John Piper and Wayne Grudem

WHEATON, ILLINOIS

50 Crucial Questions: An Overview of Central Concerns about Manhood and Womanhood

Published by Crossway
1300 Crescent Street
Wheaton, Illinois 60187

First published on its own as *50 Crucial Questions about Manhood and Womanhood*, copyright © 1992 by The Council on Biblical Manhood and Womanhood. Published earlier as "An Overview of Central Concerns: Questions and Answers," chapter 2 in *Recovering Biblical Manhood and Womanhood: A Response to Evangelical Feminism*, edited by John Piper and Wayne Grudem (Crossway), copyright © 1991, 2006 by The Council on Biblical Manhood and Womanhood.

Cover design: Dual Identity, inc.

First printing of Crossway edition 2016

Printed in the United States of America

All emphases in Scripture quotations have been added by the author.

Trade paperback ISBN: 978-1-4335-5181-9
ePub ISBN: 978-1-4335-5184-0
PDF ISBN: 978-1-4335-5182-6
Mobipocket ISBN: 978-1-4335-5183-3

Library of Congress Cataloging-in-Publication Data

Names: Piper, John, 1946– | Grudem, Wayne A.
Title: 50 crucial questions : an overview of central concerns about manhood and womanhood / John Piper and Wayne Grudem.
Other titles: Fifty crucial questions
Description: Wheaton, Illinois : Crossway, 2016. | "First published as 'An Overview of Central Concerns: Questions and Answers,' chapter 2 in Recovering Biblical Manhood and Womanhood: A Response to Evangelical Feminism, edited by John Piper and Wayne Grudem (Crossway), copyright © 1991, 2006 by The Council on Biblical Manhood and Womanhood." | Includes bibliographical references and index.
Identifiers: LCCN 2015018527 (print) | LCCN 2016004234 (ebook) | ISBN 9781433551819 (tp) | ISBN 9781433551826 (pdf) | ISBN 9781433551833 (mobi) | ISBN 9781433551840 (epub)
Subjects: LCSH: Sex role—Religious aspects—Christianity—Miscellanea.
Classification: LCC BT708 .P495 2016 (print) | LCC BT708 (ebook) | DDC 233/.5081—dc23
LC record available at http://lccn.loc.gov/2015018527

Crossway is a publishing ministry of Good News Publishers.

DP 26 25 24 23 22 21 20 19 18 17 16
14 13 12 11 10 9 8 7 6 5 4 3 2 1

Contents

Preface

This little book was originally published as chapter 2 of *Recovering Biblical Manhood and Womanhood*. We coedited that book and wrote several of the chapters, including this one.

Even as early as the 1970s, we were waving the flag of biblical complementarianism (not yet called that) over the emerging gender-leveling impulses of what was then called evangelical feminism or egalitarianism. In the decades since, the response to issues of manhood and womanhood has been neither simple nor unilateral. There is cause for joy and sorrow.

On the one hand, our culture in general has moved with stunning speed away from any Christian consensus on what is right and wrong in the matter of sexual ethics. The flashpoint has moved from male headship to homosexuality. This is no surprise to us, and you can see what we saw coming by reading question 41. The ethical and hermeneutical step from rejecting gender as a factor in what marital couples *do* to rejecting it as a factor in who marital couples *are* was a small one. If gender does not count in what the spouse *does*, then gender doesn't count in who the spouse *is*. That is where our culture has come.

On the other hand, there has been a resurgence of churches and younger Christians who take their Bibles seriously enough that they are willing to walk dramatically out of step with this culture. They see in the Bible a vision of manhood and womanhood that does not blur the sexes but puts their differences in dazzling color. These churches see the complementarian vision as life-giving for both men and women. They think this is what God has taught. And they believe God is wise and good. His ideas for sexuality are most beautiful and most satisfying.

Most important, the highlighting of male and female differences in the dynamics of marriage puts Christ and his church on display with the greatest clarity. In Ephesians 5, Paul presents the marriage of man and woman as a parable of Christ's covenant relationship with his bride, the church. The husband is to take his cues from the sacrificial leadership, protection, and provision given by Christ, and the wife is to take her cues from the clearheaded respect and glad submission that the redeemed people give to Christ.

Together, in this profoundly loving and Christ-exalting relationship, husbands and wives create outposts of an alternative kingdom in this world. In these kingdom outposts, called families, they aim to raise disciples of Jesus who are wise, bold, and risk taking. And they pray that their families will be a salty witness in a decaying society.

From the beginning, God meant for marriage to magnify the beauties of this divine-human covenant. Both egalitarianism and so-called "homosexual marriage" effectively nullify this marital parable of Christ and the church. It is gratifying to see how many younger Christians grasp the theological significance of marriage and choose to embrace the biblical vision of complementarity, lived out in thriving, mission-oriented churches.

When a person begins to take this vision seriously, questions of biblical interpretation and practical application multiply.

That is why we wrote this book. We believe that these fifty questions are as relevant today as ever. Some of them even more so. And we believe that if you follow the biblical reasoning of these questions, you will probably be able to answer others that arise by following a similar trajectory.

More than ever, we think these issues of manhood and womanhood are crucial. And as we said in the chapter that we wrote twenty-five years ago, our aim and our prayer are for the good of the church, for global mission, and for the glory of God.

Introduction

Complementarity

The issue we face in this book is how men and women should relate to each other according to the Bible. We are concerned especially with how they relate in the home and in the church. The position we take affirms the complementary differences between men and women and spells out the implications of those differences for the way men and women relate to each other in the most fulfilling way.

We defend what Larry Crabb calls "enjoying the difference," namely, that "the sexes are distinct in what they were fundamentally designed to give and in what brings them the greatest joy in relationship. . . . At the deepest level, a man serves a woman differently than a woman serves a man."[1]

We resonate with Chuck Colson when he laments the destructive tendencies of gender blending throughout our culture. We stand with him when he says, "God created two distinct types of people—male and female, masculine and feminine—with different roles and abilities for the propagation and nurturing of the race." We agree that "it assaults a basic truth of creation" when a female reporter demands access to a male locker room, when homosexual men adopt babies and use surrogate nursing bras, when female prison guards do body searches on male inmates, and when popular rock stars reverse every sexual distinction.[2]

This is why we call ourselves *complementarians*. Our vision of manhood and womanhood is shaped by a passion for reality—the beautiful reality of complementary differentiation that God designed for our joy in the beginning when God created us male and female equally in his image.

If one word must be used to describe our position, therefore, we prefer the term *complementarian*, since it suggests both equality and beneficial differences between men and women. We are uncomfortable with the term *traditionalist* because it implies an unwillingness to let Scripture challenge traditional patterns of behavior, and we certainly reject the term *hierarchicalist* because it overemphasizes structured authority while giving no suggestion of either equality or the beauty of mutual interdependence.

Lengthy volumes have been written on this issue, including our own *Recovering Biblical Manhood and Womanhood*.[3] But most people do not have time to read several books on each of the pressing issues of modern life. Often what we need are concise answers to particular questions. That is what this book is meant to offer.

50 Crucial Questions

In 1987, a group of Christian men and women, deeply concerned about certain trends both in secular society and more specifically in the evangelical religious world, formed an organization called the Council on Biblical Manhood and Womanhood (CBMW). The stated purpose of the new organization was to "set forth the teachings of the Bible about the complementary differences between men and women, created equally in the image of God, because these teachings are essential for obedience to Scripture and for the health of the family and of the church."[1]

To state publicly their concerns and goals, these Christians issued a proclamation called the *Danvers Statement* (prepared at a CBMW meeting in Danvers, Massachusetts, in December 1987). Then the newly formed Council began issuing a series of booklets addressing various aspects of biblical manhood and womanhood. In 1991, these booklets were combined with other essays and expository articles to form a 566-page volume, *Recovering Biblical Manhood and Womanhood: A Response to Evangelical Feminism*.[2] The book contains twenty-six chapters written by twenty-two men and women, and it was voted Book of the Year for 1991 by the readers of *Christianity Today*.

This short book, 50 Crucial Questions, is adapted from chapter 2 of Recovering Biblical Manhood and Womanhood. It offers an overview of the vision of manhood and womanhood presented in the larger volume by giving cogent summary responses to the most common objections to that vision. Because every effort to answer one question (on any important issue) begets new questions, the list of questions here is not exhaustive. Nonetheless, we hope to give enough trajectories that readers can track the flight of our intention to its appointed target: the good of the church, global mission, and the glory of God.

1. Why do you regard the issue of male and female roles as so important?

We are concerned not merely with the behavioral roles of men and women but also with the underlying natures of manhood and womanhood themselves. Biblical truth and clarity in this matter are important because error and confusion over sexual identity lead to (1) marriage patterns that do not portray the relationship between Christ and the church[3] (Eph. 5:31–32); (2) parenting practices that do not train boys to be masculine or girls to be feminine; (3) homosexual tendencies and increasing attempts to justify homosexual alliances (see question 41); and (4) patterns of unbiblical female leadership in the church that reflect and promote the confusion over the true meaning of manhood and womanhood.

God's gift of complementary manhood and womanhood was exhilarating from the beginning (Gen. 2:23). It is precious beyond estimation. But today it is esteemed lightly and is vanishing from much of modern society. We believe that what is at stake in human sexuality is the very fabric of life as God wills it to be for the holiness of his people and for their saving mission to the world. (See the "Rationale" of the *Danvers Statement* at the end of this book.)

2. What do you mean by "unbiblical female leadership in the church" (in question 1)?

We are persuaded that the Bible teaches that only men should be pastors and elders. That is, men should bear primary responsibility for Christlike leadership and teaching in the church. So we believe it is unbiblical, and therefore detrimental, for women to assume this role. (See question 13.)

3. Where in the Bible do you get the idea that only men should be the pastors and elders of the church?

The most explicit texts relating directly to the leadership of men in the church are 1 Timothy 2:11–15; 1 Corinthians 11:2–16; 14:34–36. Chapters 5, 6, and 9 of *Recovering Biblical Manhood and Womanhood* present detailed exegetical support for why we believe these texts give abiding sanction to an eldership of spiritual men. Moreover, the biblical connection between family and church strongly suggests that the headship of the husband at home leads naturally to the primary leadership of spiritual men in the church.

4. What about marriage? What do you mean by "marriage patterns that do not portray the relationship between Christ and the church" (in question 1)?

We believe the Bible teaches that God intends the relationship between husband and wife to portray the relationship between Christ and his church. The husband is to model the loving, sacrificial leadership of Christ, and the wife is to model the glad submission offered freely by the church. (For more, see chapter 13 in *Recovering Biblical Manhood and Womanhood.*)

5. What do you mean by "submission" (in question 4)?

Submission refers to a wife's divine calling to honor and affirm her husband's leadership and help carry it through according to her gifts. It is not an absolute surrender of her will. Rather, we speak of her *disposition to yield* to her husband's guidance and her *inclination* to follow his leadership. Her absolute authority is Christ, not her husband. She submits "out of reverence for Christ" (Eph. 5:21). The supreme authority of Christ qualifies the authority of her husband. She should never follow her husband into sin. Nevertheless, even when she may have to stand with Christ against the sinful will of her husband (e.g., 1 Pet. 3:1, where she does not yield to her husband's unbelief), she can still have a *spirit* of submission—a *disposition* to yield. She can show by her attitude and behavior that she does not like resisting his will and that she longs for him to forsake sin and lead in righteousness so that her disposition to honor him as head can again produce harmony.

6. What do you mean when you call the husband "head" (in question 5)?

In the home, biblical headship refers to the husband's divine calling to take primary responsibility for Christlike leadership, protection, and provision. (See question 13 on the meaning of "primary.")

7. Where in the Bible do you get the idea that husbands should be the leaders in their homes?

The most explicit texts relating directly to headship and submission in marriage are Genesis 1–3; Ephesians 5:21–33; Colossians 3:18–19; 1 Timothy 3:2, 4, 12; Titus 2:5; and 1 Peter 3:1–7.

In view of these teaching passages, the pattern of male leadership that pervades the biblical portrait of family life probably reflects not merely a cultural phenomenon over thousands of years but God's original design, even though corrupted by sin. *Recovering Biblical Manhood and Womanhood* gives detailed exegetical support for why we believe these passages teach that headship includes primary leadership, which is the responsibility of the man.

8. When you say that a wife should not follow her husband into sin (question 5), what's left of headship? Who is to say what act of his leadership is sinful enough to justify her refusal to follow?

We are not claiming to live without ambiguities, because sometimes people face difficult decisions in complicated situations. Neither are we saying that headship consists in a series of directives to the wife. Leadership is not synonymous with unilateral decision making. In fact, in a good marriage, leadership consists mainly in taking responsibility to establish a pattern of interaction that honors both husband and wife (and children) as a store of varied wisdom for family life. Headship bears the primary responsibility for the moral design and planning in the home, but the development of that design and plan will include the wife (who may be wiser and more intelligent). None of this is nullified by some ambiguities in difficult, borderline cases where husbands and wives disagree on what constitutes faithfulness to Christ.

The leadership structures of state, church, and home do not become meaningless even though Christ alone is the absolute authority over each one. The New Testament command for us to submit to church leaders (Heb. 13:17) is not meaningless, even though we are told that elders will arise speaking perverse things (Acts 20:30) and that when they do so, they should be rebuked rather than followed (1 Tim. 5:20). The command to submit to civil authorities (Rom. 13:1) is not meaningless, even though there is such a thing as conscientious objection (Acts 5:29). Nor is the reality of a man's gentle, strong leadership at home nullified just because his wife must ultimately submit to Christ's authority, not his. In the cases where his leadership fails to win her glad response, he must entrust himself to the grace of God and seek the path of biblical wisdom through prayer and counsel. None of us escapes the (sometimes agonizing) ambiguities of real life.

9. Don't you think that stressing headship and submission gives impetus to the epidemic of wife abuse?

No. First, we stress Christlike, sacrificial headship that keeps the good of the wife in view and regards her as a joint heir of the grace of life (1 Pet. 3:7), and at the same time, we stress thoughtful submission that does not make the husband an absolute lord (see question 5). Second, we believe that wife abuse (and husband abuse) have some deep roots in the failure of parents to impart to their sons and daughters the meaning of true masculinity and true femininity. The confusions and frustrations of sexual identity often explode in harmful behaviors. The solution is not to minimize gender differences (which will then break out in menacing ways) but to teach in the home and the church how true manhood and womanhood express themselves in the loving and complementary roles of marriage.

10. But don't you believe in "mutual submission," which Paul seems to teach in Ephesians 5:21 ("submitting to one another")?

Everything depends on what you mean by "mutual submission." Some of us put more stress on reciprocity here than others.[4]

But even if Paul means complete reciprocity (wives submit to husbands and husbands submit to wives), this does not mean that husbands and wives should submit to each other *in the same way*. The key is to remember that in this very passage the relationship between husband and wife follows the pattern of the relationship between Christ and the church. Do Christ and the church mutually submit to each other? They do *not* if submission means Christ yields to the authority of the church. But they do if submission means that Christ submitted himself to suffering and death for the good of the church. That, however, is not how the church submits to Christ. The church submits to Christ by affirming his authority and following his lead. So mutual submission does not mean submitting to each other *in the same ways*. Therefore, mutual submission does not compromise Christ's headship over the church, and it should not compromise the headship of a husband over his wife. (For the ways in which Scripture places parameters on the husband's exercise of headship, see question 36.)

11. If "head" means "source" in Ephesians 5:23 ("the husband is the head of the wife"), as some scholars say it does, wouldn't that change your whole way of seeing this passage and eliminate the idea of the husband's leadership in the home?

No. But before we deal with this hypothetical possibility, we should say that the meaning "source" in Ephesians 5:23 is very unlikely. Scholars will want to read the extensive treatment of this word in appendix 1 of *Recovering Biblical Manhood and Womanhood* and in appendices 3 and 4 of *Evangelical Feminism and Biblical Truth*.[5] But realistically, laypeople will draw their conclusion on the basis of what makes sense here in Ephesians. Verse 23 is the ground, or argument, for verse 22; thus it begins with the word *for*: "Wives, submit to your own husbands as to the Lord. For the husband is the head of the wife." When the headship of the husband is given as the *ground* for the submission of the wife, the most natural understanding is that headship signifies some kind of leadership.

Moreover, Paul has a picture in his mind when he says that the husband is the head of the wife. The word *head* does not dangle in space waiting for any meaning to be assigned to it. Paul says, "For the husband is the head of the wife even as Christ is the head of the church, *his body*" (Eph. 5:23). The picture in Paul's mind is of a body with a head. This is very important because it leads to the "one flesh" unity of husband and wife in the following verses. A head and its body are "one flesh." Thus Paul goes on to say in verses 28–30, "In this same way husbands should love their wives as their own bodies. He who loves his wife loves himself. For no one ever hated his own flesh, but nourishes and cherishes it, just as Christ does the church, because we are members of his body." Paul carries through the image of Christ the head and the church his body. Christ nourishes and cherishes the church because we are limbs of his body. So the husband is like a head to his wife, so that when he nourishes and cherishes her, he is really nourishing and cherishing himself, as the head who is "one flesh" with this body.

We find it significant that in all of ancient Greek literature, one person is called the "head" (Greek *kephalē*) of another person or a group in more than forty examples, and in every single instance the person who is called the "head" is in a position of authority over the other person or the group.[6] In no example is the person who is called the "head" the "source" of the other person or group. So this meaning remains highly suspect, with no clear examples to support it.

But even if "head" were to mean "source" in Ephesians 5:23, what is the husband the source of? What does the body get from the head? It gets nourishment (that's mentioned in v. 29). And we can understand that, because the mouth is in the head and because nourishment comes through the mouth to the body. But that's not all the body gets from the head. It gets guidance, because the eyes are in the head. And it gets alertness and protection, because the ears are in the head. And it gets direction and governance, because the brain is in the head.

In other words, if the husband as head is one flesh with the wife, his body, and if he is therefore a source of guidance, food, and alertness, then the natural conclusion is that the head, the husband, has a primary responsibility for leadership, provision, and protection. So even if you give "head" the meaning "source," the most natural interpretation of these verses is that husbands are called by God to take primary responsibility for Christlike servant-leadership, protection, and provision in the home, and wives are called to honor and affirm their husbands' leadership and help carry it through according to their gifts.[7]

12. Isn't your stress on leadership in the church and headship in the home contrary to the emphasis of Christ in Luke 22:26, "Let the greatest among you become as the youngest, and the leader as one who serves"?

No. We are trying to hold precisely these two things in biblical balance, namely, leadership and servanthood. It would be contrary to Christ if we said that servanthood cancels out leadership. Jesus is not dismantling leadership; he is defining it. The very word he uses for "leader" in Luke 22:26 is used in Hebrews 13:17, which says, "Obey your *leaders* and submit to them, for they are keeping watch over your souls, as those who will have to give an account." Leaders are to be servants in sacrificially caring for the souls of the people. But this does not make them less than leaders, as we see in the words *obey* and *submit*. Jesus was no less a leader of the disciples when he was on his knees washing their feet than when he was giving them the Great Commission.

13. In questions 2 and 6, you said that the calling of the man is to bear "primary responsibility" for leadership in the church and the home. What do you mean by "primary"?

We mean that there are levels and kinds of leadership for which women may and often should take responsibility. There are kinds of teaching, administration, organization, ministry, influence, and initiative that wives should undertake at home and women should undertake at church. Male headship at home and male eldership at church mean that men bear the responsibility for the overall patterns of life, even while headship does not prescribe the details of who does precisely what activity. Thus, after the fall, God called Adam to account first (Gen. 3:9), not because the woman bore no responsibility for sin but because the man bore primary responsibility for life in the garden—including sin.

14. If the husband is to treat his wife as Christ does the church, does that mean he should govern all the details of her life and that she should clear all her actions with him?

No. We may not press the analogy between Christ and the husband that far. Unlike Christ, all husbands sin. They are finite and fallible in their wisdom. Not only that, but also, unlike Christ, a husband is preparing a bride not merely for himself but also for another, namely, Christ. He does not merely act *as* Christ;

he also acts *for* Christ. At this point, he must not be Christ to his wife, lest he be a traitor to Christ. He must lead in such a way that his wife is encouraged to depend on Christ and not on himself.

Practically, that rules out belittling supervision and fastidious oversight. Even when acting as Christ, the husband must remember that Christ leads the church not as his daughter but as his wife. He is preparing her to be a "fellow heir," not a servant girl (Rom. 8:17). Any kind of leadership that, in the name of Christlike headship, tends to foster in a wife personal immaturity or spiritual weakness or insecurity through excessive control, picky supervision, or oppressive domination has missed the point of the analogy in Ephesians 5. Christ does not create that kind of wife.

15. Don't you think that these texts are examples of temporary compromise with the patriarchal status quo, while the main thrust of Scripture is toward the leveling of gender-based role differences?

We recognize that Scripture sometimes regulates undesirable relationships without condoning them as permanent ideals. For example, Jesus said to the Pharisees, "Because of your hardness of heart Moses allowed you to divorce your wives, but from the beginning it was not so" (Matt. 19:8). Another example is the regulation of how Christian slaves were to relate to their masters, even though Paul longed for every slave to be received by his master "no longer as a bondservant but more than a bondservant, as a beloved brother" (Philem. 16).

But we do not put the loving headship of husbands or the godly eldership of men in the same category with divorce or slavery. The reason we don't is threefold:

1. Male and female personhood, with some corresponding role distinctions, is rooted in God's act of creation (Genesis 1 and 2) before the sinful distortions of the status quo were established (Genesis 3). This argument is the same one, we believe, that evangelical feminists would use to defend heterosexual marriage against the (increasingly prevalent) argument that the "leveling thrust" of the Bible leads *properly* to homosexual alliances. They would say, "No, because the leveling thrust of the Bible is not meant to dismantle the created order of nature." That is our fundamental argument as well.
2. The redemptive thrust of the Bible does not aim at abolishing headship and submission but at restoring them to their original purposes in the created order.
3. The Bible contains no indictments of loving headship and gives no encouragement to forsake it. Therefore, it is wrong to portray the Bible as overwhelmingly egalitarian with a few contextually relativized patriarchal texts. The contraheadship thrust of Scripture simply does not exist. It *seems* to exist only when Scripture's aim to redeem headship and submission is portrayed as undermining them. (See question 50 for an example of this hermeneutical flaw.)

16. Aren't the arguments made to defend the exclusion of women from the pastorate today parallel to the arguments Christians made to defend slavery in the nineteenth century?

See question 15 for the beginning of our answer to this problem. To go a little further, the preservation of marriage is not parallel with the preservation of slavery. The existence of slavery is not rooted in any creation ordinance, but the existence of marriage is. Paul's regulations for how slaves and masters should relate to each other do not assume the goodness of the institution of slavery. Rather, seeds for slavery's dissolution were sown in Philemon 16 ("no longer as a bondservant but more than a bondservant, as a beloved brother"), Ephesians 6:9 ("Masters, . . . stop your threatening [toward your bondservants]"), Colossians 4:1 ("Masters, treat your bondservants justly and fairly"), and 1 Timothy 6:1–2 (masters and bondservants are "brothers"). Where these seeds of equality came to full flower, the very institution of slavery would cease. In fact, when 1 Timothy 1:10 is understood correctly, it absolutely prohibits involuntary servitude, for it lists "enslavers" among a list of people who are "ungodly and sinners" (v. 9).

But Paul's regulations for how husbands and wives relate to each other in marriage *do* assume the goodness of the institution of marriage—and not only its goodness but also its foundation in the will of the Creator from the beginning of time (Eph. 5:31–32). Moreover, Paul locates the foundation of marriage in the will of God at creation in a way that shows that his regulations for marriage also flow from this created order. He quotes Genesis 2:24, "they shall become one flesh," and explains, "I am saying that it refers to Christ and the church." From this "mystery," he draws out the pattern of the relationship between the husband as head (on the analogy of Christ) and the wife as his body or flesh (on the analogy of the church) and derives the appropriateness of the husband's leadership and the wife's submission. Thus Paul's *regulations* concerning marriage are just as rooted in the created order as is *the institution itself*. This is not true of slavery. Therefore, while some slave owners in the nineteenth century admittedly argued in ways parallel with our defense of distinct roles in marriage, the parallel was superficial and misguided. Those who attempted to defend slavery from the Bible were clearly wrong in their interpretations, and they decisively lost the argument.

Mary Stewart Van Leeuwen points out from 1 Timothy 6:1–6 that according to the nineteenth-century Christian supporters of slavery, "even though the institution of slavery did not go back to creation . . . the fact that Paul based its maintenance on a revelation from Jesus himself meant that anyone wishing to abolish slavery (or even improve the slaves' working conditions) was defying timeless Biblical norms for society."[8] The problem with this argument is that Paul uses the teachings of Jesus not to "maintain" the institution of slavery but to regulate the behavior of Christian slaves and masters in an institution that already existed in part because of sin. What Jesus endorses is the kind of inner freedom and love that is willing to go the extra mile in service, even when the demand is unjust (Matt. 5:41). Therefore, it is wrong to say that the words of Jesus give a foundation for slavery in the same way that creation gives a foundation for marriage. Jesus does not give any foundation for slavery, but creation gives an unshakable foundation for marriage and for the complementary roles of husband and wife.

Finally, if those who ask this question are concerned to avoid the mistakes of Christians who defended slavery, we must remember the real possibility that it is not complementarians but evangelical feminists who today resemble nineteenth-century defenders of slavery in the most significant way: using arguments from the Bible to justify conformity to some very strong pressures in contemporary society (in favor of slavery then and feminism now).

17. Since the New Testament teaching on the submission of wives in marriage is found in the part of Scripture known as the "household codes" (*Haustafeln*), which were taken over

in part from first-century culture, shouldn't we recognize that what Scripture is teaching us is not to offend against current culture but to fit in with it up to a point and thus be willing to change our practices of how men and women relate, rather than hold fast to a temporary first-century pattern?

This is a more sophisticated form of the kind of questions already asked in questions 15 and 16. A few additional comments may be helpful. First, by way of explanation, the "household codes" refer to Ephesians 5:22–6:9, Colossians 3:18–4:1, and, less exactly, 1 Peter 2:13–3:7, passages that include instructions for pairs of household members: wives and husbands, children and parents, and slaves and masters.

The first problem with this argument is that the parallels to these "household codes" in the surrounding world are not very close to what we have in the New Testament. It is not at all as though Paul simply took over either content or form from his culture. Both are very different from the nonbiblical "parallels" that we know of.[9]

The second problem with this argument is that it maximizes what is incidental (the little that Paul's teaching has in common with the surrounding world) and minimizes what is utterly crucial (the radically Christian nature and foundation of what Paul teaches concerning marriage in the "household codes"). We have shown in questions 15 and 16 that Paul is hardly unreflective in saying some things that are superficially similar to the surrounding culture. He bases his teaching of headship on the nature of Christ's relation to the church, which he sees "mysteriously" revealed in Genesis 2:24 and thus in creation itself.

We do not think that it honors the integrity of Paul or the inspiration of Scripture to claim that Paul resorted to arguing that his exhortations were rooted in the very order of creation and in the work of Christ in order to justify his sanctioning temporary accommodations to his culture. It is far more likely that the theological depth and divine inspiration of the apostle led him not only to be very discriminating in what he took over from the world but also to sanction his ethical commands with creation only where they had abiding validity. Thus we believe that there is good reason to affirm the enduring applicability of Paul's pattern for marriage: Let the husband, as head of the home, love and lead as Christ does the church, and let the wife affirm that loving leadership as the church honors Christ.

18. But what about the liberating way Jesus treated women? Doesn't he explode our hierarchical traditions and open the way for women to be given access to all ministry roles?

We believe the ministry of Jesus has revolutionary implications for the way sinful men and women treat each other. His care for women was frequently evident: "And ought not this woman, a daughter of Abraham whom Satan bound for eighteen years, be loosed from this bond?" (Luke 13:16). Everything Jesus taught and did was an attack on the pride that makes men and women belittle each other. Everything he taught and did was a summons to the humility and love that purge self-exaltation out of leadership and servility out of submission. He put man's lustful look in the category of adultery and threatened it with hell (Matt. 5:28–29). He condemned the whimsical disposing of women in divorce (Matt. 19:8–9). He called us to account for every careless word we utter (Matt. 12:36). He commanded that we treat each other the way we would like to be treated (Matt. 7:12). He said to the callous chief priests, "Prostitutes go into the kingdom of God before you" (Matt. 21:31). He was accompanied by women, he taught women, and women bore witness to his resurrection life. Against every social custom that demeans or abuses men and women, the words of Jesus can be applied: "And why do you break the commandment of God for the sake of your tradition?" (Matt. 15:3).

But where does Jesus say or do anything that criticizes the order of creation in which men bear a primary responsibility to lead, protect, and sustain? Nowhere did he call this good order into question. It simply does not follow to say that since women ministered to Jesus and learned from Jesus and ran to tell the disciples that Jesus was risen, this must mean that Jesus opposed the loving headship of husbands or the limitation of eldership to spiritual men. We would not argue that merely because Jesus chose twelve men to be his authoritative apostles, Jesus must have favored an eldership of only men in the church. But this argument would be at least as valid as arguing that anything else Jesus did means he would oppose an eldership of all men or the headship of husbands. The effort to show that the ministry of Jesus is part of a major biblical thrust against gender-based roles can only be sustained by assuming (rather than demonstrating) that he meant to nullify headship and submission rather than rectify them. What is clear is that Jesus radically purged leadership of pride and fear and self-exaltation and that he also radically honored women as persons worthy of the highest respect under God.

19. Doesn't the significant role women had in ministry with Paul show that his teachings do not mean that women should be excluded from ministry?

Yes. But the issue is not whether women should be excluded from ministry. They shouldn't be. There are hundreds of ministries open to men and women. We must pose our questions more carefully. Otherwise, we obscure the truth from the start.

The issue here is whether any of the women serving with Paul in ministry fulfilled roles that would be inconsistent with a limitation of the eldership to men. We believe the answer to that question is *no*. Tom Schreiner has dealt with this matter more fully in chapter 11 of *Recovering Biblical Manhood and Womanhood*. But we can perhaps illustrate the matter with two significant women in Paul's ministry.

Paul said that Euodia and Syntyche "labored side by side with me in the gospel together with Clement and the rest of my fellow workers" (Phil. 4:2–3). There is wonderful honor given to Euodia and Syntyche here for their ministry with Paul. But there are no compelling grounds for affirming that the nature of the ministry was contrary to the limitations that Paul set forth in 1 Timothy 2:12. One must *assume* this contrariety in order to make a case against these limitations. Paul would surely say that both the "overseers" *and* the "deacons" mentioned in Philippians 1:1 were fellow workers with him when he was there. And that means one can be a "fellow worker" with Paul without holding a position of authority over men. (We are assuming from 1 Timothy 3:2 and 5:17 that what distinguishes an elder from a deacon is that the responsibility for teaching and governance was the elder's and not the deacon's.)

Paul praises Phoebe as a "servant" or "deacon" of the church at Cenchreae since, as he puts it, she "has been a patron of many and of myself as well" (Rom. 16:1–2). Some have tried to argue that the Greek word behind "patron" really means "leader."[10] This is doubtful, since it is hard to imagine, on any account, what Paul would mean by saying that Phoebe became his leader.

He could, of course, mean that she was an influential patroness who gave sanctuary to him and his band or that she used her community influence for the cause of the gospel and for Paul in particular. She was a very significant person and played a crucial role in the ministry. But to derive anything from this term that is contrary to our understanding of 1 Timothy 2:12, one would have to *assume* that Phoebe exercised authority over men. The text simply doesn't show that.

20. But Priscilla taught Apollos, didn't she (Acts 18:26)? And she is even mentioned before her husband, Aquila. Doesn't that show that the practice of the early church did not exclude women from the teaching office of the church?

We are eager to affirm Priscilla as a fellow worker with Paul in Christ (Rom. 16:3)! She and her husband were very influential in the church in Corinth (1 Cor. 16:19), as well as in Ephesus. We can think of many women in our churches today like Priscilla. Nothing in our understanding of Scripture says that when a husband and wife visit an unbeliever (or a confused believer—or anyone else), the wife must be silent. It is easy for us to imagine the dynamics of such a discussion in which Priscilla contributes to the explanation and illustration of baptism in Jesus's name and the work of the Holy Spirit. This dynamic is significantly different from the public, authoritative teaching of Scripture to a congregation that Paul prohibits for women in 1 Timothy 2:12.

What is fitting for men and women in that kind of setting? We don't want to oversimplify it or issue an artificial list of rules for what the woman and the man can say and do. Rather, such a scenario calls for the delicate and sensitive preservation of personal dynamics that honor the headship of Aquila without squelching the wisdom and insight of Priscilla. There is nothing in this text that cannot be explained by this understanding of what happened.

We do not claim to know the spirit and balance of how Priscilla and Aquila and Apollos related to each other. We only claim that a feminist reconstruction of the relationship has no more warrant than ours. The right of Priscilla to hold an authoritative teaching office cannot be built on an event about which we know so little. It is only a guess to suggest that the order of their names signifies Priscilla's leadership. Luke may simply have wanted to give greater honor to the woman by putting her name first (1 Pet. 3:7) or may have had another reason unknown to us. Saying that Priscilla illustrates the authoritative teaching of women in the New Testament is the kind of precarious and unwarranted inference that is made again and again by evangelical feminists and then called a major biblical thrust against gender-based role distinctions. But many invalid inferences do not make a major thrust.

21. Are you saying that it is all right for women to teach men under some circumstances?

When Paul says in 1 Timothy 2:12, "I do not permit a woman to teach or to exercise authority over a man; rather, she is to remain quiet," we do not understand him to mean an absolute prohibition of all teaching by women. Elsewhere, Paul instructs the older women to "teach what is good, and so train the young women" (Titus 2:3–4), and he commends the teaching that Eunice and Lois gave to their respective son and grandson Timothy (2 Tim. 1:5; 3:14). Proverbs praises the ideal wife because "she opens her mouth with wisdom, and the teaching of kindness is on her tongue" (Prov. 31:26). Paul endorses women prophesying in church (1 Cor. 11:5) and says that men "learn" by such prophesying (1 Cor. 14:31) and that the members (presumably men and women) should be "teaching and admonishing one another in all wisdom, singing psalms and hymns and spiritual songs" (Col. 3:16). Then, of course, there is Priscilla at Aquila's side correcting Apollos (Acts 18:26).

It is arbitrary to think that Paul had every form of teaching in mind in 1 Timothy 2:12. *Teaching* and *learning* are such broad terms that it is *impossible* that women not teach men and that men not learn from women *in some sense*. There is even a way that nature teaches (1 Cor. 11:14) and a fig tree teaches (Matt. 24:32) and suffering teaches (Heb. 5:8) and human behavior teaches (1 Cor. 4:6; 1 Pet. 3:1).

If Paul did not have every conceivable form of teaching and learning in mind, what did he mean? First, it helps to identify the setting; here the church is assembled for prayer and teaching (1 Tim. 2:8–10; 3:15). Second, perhaps the best clue is the coupling of "teaching" with "exercising authority over men." We would say that the teaching inappropriate for a woman is the teaching of men in settings or ways that dishonor the calling of men to bear the primary responsibility for teaching and leadership. This primary responsibility is to be carried by the pastors or elders. Therefore, we think it is God's will that only men bear the responsibility for these offices.

22. Can't a pastor authorize a woman to teach Scripture to the congregation and then continue to exercise oversight while she teaches?

It is right for all the teaching ministries of the church to meet with the approval of the guardians and overseers (i.e., elders) of the church. However, it would be wrong for the leadership of the church to use its authority to sanction the de facto functioning of a woman as a teaching elder in the church, only without the name. In other words, to biblically affirm a woman teaching, two kinds of criteria should be met. One is to have the endorsement of the spiritual overseers of the church (i.e., elders). The other is to avoid contexts and kinds of teaching that put a woman in the position of functioning as the de facto spiritual shepherd of a group of men or to avoid the kind of teaching that by its very nature calls for strong, forceful pressing of men's consciences on the basis of divine authority. These actions would violate what Paul says in 1 Timothy 2:12. A pastor cannot rightfully give permission to do something that Scripture forbids, for pastors do not have higher authority than Scripture itself.

23. How can you be in favor of women prophesying in church but not in favor of women being pastors and elders? Isn't prophecy at the very heart of those roles?

No. The role of pastor/elder is primarily governance and teaching (1 Tim. 5:17). In the list of qualifications for elders, the prophetic gift is not mentioned, but the ability to teach is (1 Tim. 3:2). In Ephesians 4:11, prophets are distinguished from pastor-teachers. And even though men learn from prophecies that women give, Paul distinguishes the gift of prophecy from the gift of teaching (Rom. 12:6–7; 1 Cor. 12:28). Women are nowhere forbidden to prophesy. Paul simply regulates the demeanor in which they prophesy so as not to compromise the principle of the spiritual leadership of men (1 Cor. 11:5–10).

Prophecy in the worship of the early church was not the kind of authoritative, infallible revelation we associate with the written prophecies of the Old Testament.[11] It was a report in human words based on a spontaneous, personal revelation from the Holy Spirit (1 Cor. 14:30) for the purpose of edification, encouragement, consolation, conviction, and guidance (1 Cor. 14:3, 24–25; Acts 21:4; 16:6–10). It was not necessarily free from a mixture of human error and thus required assessment (1 Thess. 5:20–21; 1 Cor. 14:29) on the basis of the apostolic (biblical) teaching (1 Cor. 14:36–38; 2 Thess. 2:1–3). Prophecy in the early church did not correspond to the sermon today or to a formal exposition of Scripture. Both women and men could stand and "prophesy"—that is, share what they believed God had brought to mind for the good of the church. But the public testing of these words and the regular Bible teaching ministry was the responsibility of the elder-teachers. This latter role is the one Paul assigns uniquely to men.[12]

24. Are you saying, then, that you accept the freedom of women to prophesy publicly as described in Acts 2:17; 21:9; and 1 Corinthians 11:5?

Yes.[13]

25. Since it says in 1 Corinthians 14:34 that "women should keep silent in the churches," it doesn't seem like your position is really biblical because of how much speaking you really do allow to women. How do you account for this straightforward prohibition of women speaking?

The reason we believe Paul does not mean for women to be *totally* silent in the church is that in 1 Corinthians 11:5 he permits women to pray and prophesy in church: "Every wife who *prays* or *prophesies* with her head uncovered dishonors her head." But someone may ask, "Why do you choose to let 1 Corinthians 11:5 limit the meaning of 1 Corinthians 14:34 rather than the other way around?"

To begin our answer, we notice in both 1 Corinthians 14:35

and 1 Corinthians 11:6 that Paul is concerned about what is "shameful" or "disgraceful" for women (the Greek word in both verses is *aischron*, which in the New Testament appears only in 1 Corinthians). The issue is not whether women are competent or intelligent or wise or well taught. The issue is how they relate to the men of the church. In 1 Corinthians 14:34 Paul speaks of *submission*, and in 1 Corinthians 11:3 he speaks of man as *head*. So the issue of shamefulness is at root an issue of doing something that would dishonor the role of the men as leaders of the congregation. If *all* speaking were shameful in this way, then Paul could not have condoned a woman's praying and prophesying, as he does in 1 Corinthians 11:5 precisely when the issue of shamefulness is what is at stake. But Paul shows in 1 Corinthians 11:5–16 that what is at stake is not *that* women are praying and prophesying in public but *how* they are doing it. That is, are they doing it with the dress and demeanor that signify their affirmation of the headship of the men who are called to lead the church?

In a similar way, we look into the context of 1 Corinthians 14:33–36 to find similar clues for the *kind* of speaking Paul may have in mind when he says it is "shameful" for a woman to speak. We notice again that the issue is not the ability or the wisdom of women to speak intelligently but how women are relating to men (*hypotassesthōsan*—"let them be in submission"). Some kind of interaction is taking place that Paul thinks compromises the calling of the men to be the primary leaders of the church. Chapter 6 of *Recovering Biblical Manhood and Womanhood* argues in detail that the inappropriate interaction relates to the testing of prophecies referred to in 1 Corinthians 14:29. Women are taking a role here that Paul thinks is inappropriate, and so it's in this activity of public judgment on spoken prophecies that he calls them to be silent.[14] In other words, in both 1 Corinthians 11 and 1 Corinthians 14 Paul is calling for not the total silence of women but a kind of involvement that signifies, in various ways, their glad affirmation of the leadership of the men God has called to be the guardians and overseers of the flock.

26. Doesn't Paul's statement that "there is no male and female, for you are all one in Christ Jesus" (Gal. 3:28) take away gender as a basis for distinction of roles in the church?

No. Most evangelicals still agree that this text is not a warrant for homosexuality. In other words, most of us do not force Paul's "neither male nor female" beyond what we know from other passages he would approve. For example, we know from Romans 1:24–32 that Paul does not mean for the teaching in Galatians 3:28 to overthrow the created order of different male and female roles in sexual relations.

The context of Galatians 3:28 makes abundantly clear the sense in which men and women are equal in Christ: they are equally justified by faith (v. 24), equally free from the bondage of legalism (v. 25), equally children of God (v. 26), equally clothed with Christ (v. 27), equally possessed by Christ (v. 29), and equally heirs of the promises to Abraham (v. 29).

This last blessing is especially significant, namely, women's equality of being fellow heirs with men of God's promises. In 1 Peter 3:1–7, the blessing of being joint heirs "of the grace of life" (v. 7) is connected with the exhortation for women to submit to their husbands (v. 1) and for their husbands to treat their wives with respect "as the weaker vessel" (v. 7). In other words, Peter saw no conflict between the neither-male-nor-female principle regarding our inheritance and the headship-submission principle regarding our roles. Galatians 3:28 does not abolish gender-based roles established by God and redeemed by Christ.

Finally, it is important to pay careful attention to what Paul actually says in Galatians 3:28. He does not say, "you are all *the same* in Christ Jesus," but, "you are all *one* in Christ Jesus." He is stressing their unity in Christ, not their sameness.

27. How do you explain God's apparent endorsement of Old Testament women who had prophetic or leadership roles?

First, we keep in mind that God has no antipathy toward revealing his will to women. Nor does he pronounce them unreliable messengers. The differentiation of roles for men and women in ministry is rooted not in women's incompetence to receive or transmit truth but in the primary responsibility of men in God's order to lead and teach. The instances of women who prophesied and led do not call this order into question. Rather, there are pointers in each case that the women either endorsed and honored the usual leadership of men or indicted men's failures to lead.

For example, Miriam, the prophetess, focused her ministry, as far as we can tell, on the women of Israel (Ex. 15:20). Deborah, a prophetess, judge, and mother in Israel (Judg. 4:4; 5:7), as with Jael (Judg. 5:24–27), was a living indictment of the weakness of Barak and other men in Israel who should have been more courageous leaders (Judg. 4:9). (The period of the judges is an especially precarious foundation for building a vision of God's ideal for leadership. In those days, God was not averse to bringing about states of affairs that did not conform to his revealed will in order to achieve some wise purpose [cf. Judg. 14:4].)

Similarly, Huldah evidently exercised her prophetic gift not in a public preaching ministry but by means of private consultation (2 Kings 22:14–20). And Anna, the prophetess at the beginning of the New Testament, filled her days with fasting and prayer in the temple (Luke 2:36–37).

We must also keep in mind that God's granting power or revelation to a person is no sure sign that this person is an ideal model for us to follow in every respect. This is evident, for example, from the fact that some of those whom God blessed in the Old Testament were polygamists (e.g., Abraham and David). Not even the gift of prophecy is proof of a person's obedience and endorsement by God. As strange as this sounds, 1 Samuel 19:23–24, Matthew 7:22, and 1 Corinthians 13:2 show that this is so. Moreover, with each woman referred to above, we have an instance of a charismatic emergence on the scene, not an installation to the ordinary Old Testament office of priest, which was the responsibility of men.

28. Do you think women are more gullible than men?

In 1 Timothy 2:14 we read, "Adam was not deceived, but the woman was deceived and became a transgressor." Paul gives this as one of the reasons why he does not permit women "to teach or to exercise authority over a man" (v. 12). Historically, this has usually been taken to mean that women in general are more gullible or deceivable than men and therefore less fit for the doctrinal oversight of the church.

This interpretation may, in a way, be correct (see question 29). However, we are attracted to another understanding of Paul's argument. We think that Satan's main target was not Eve's peculiar gullibility (if that was in fact true of her) but rather Adam's headship as the one ordained by God to be responsible for the life of the garden. Satan's subtlety is that he knew the created order God had ordained for the good of the family, and he deliberately defied it by ignoring the man and taking up his dealings with the woman. Satan put her in the position of spokesman, leader, and defender. At that moment, both the man and the woman slipped from their innocence and let themselves be drawn into a pattern of relating to each other that to this day has proved destructive.

If this is the proper understanding, then what Paul meant in 1 Timothy 2:14 was this: "Adam was not deceived (that is, Adam was not approached by the deceiver and did not carry on direct dealings with the deceiver), but the woman was deceived and became a transgressor (that is, she was the one who took up dealings with the deceiver and was led through her direct interaction with him into deception and transgression)." In this case, the main point is not that the man is undeceivable or that the woman is more deceivable but that when God's order of leadership is repudiated, it brings damage and ruin. Men and women are both more vulnerable to error and sin when they forsake the order that God has intended.

29. But it does look as if Paul really thought Eve was somehow more vulnerable to deception than Adam. Wouldn't this make Paul a culpable chauvinist?

No. When someone asks if women are weaker than men or smarter than men or more easily frightened than men or something like that, perhaps the best way to answer is this: women are weaker in some ways and men are weaker in others; women are smarter in some ways and men are smarter in others; women are more easily frightened in some circumstances and men are more easily frightened in others. It is dangerous to put negative values on the so-called weaknesses that each of us has. God intends for all the "weaknesses" that characteristically belong to the man to call forth and highlight the woman's strengths. And God intends for all the "weaknesses" that characteristically belong to the woman to call forth and highlight the man's strengths.

Even if 1 Timothy 2:14 meant that in some circumstances women are characteristically more vulnerable to deception, that would not settle anything about the equality or worth of manhood and womanhood. Boasting in either sex as superior to the other is folly. Men and women, as God created us, are different in hundreds of ways. Being created equally in the image of God means at least this: that when the so-called weakness and strength columns for manhood and for womanhood are added up, the value at the bottom is going to be the same for each. And when you take those two columns and put them on top of each other, God intends them to be the perfect complement to each other.

30. If a woman is not allowed to teach men in a regular, official way, why is it permissible for her to teach children, who are far more impressionable and defenseless?

This question assumes something that we do not believe. As we implied in question 21, we do not build our vision on the assumption that the Bible assigns women their role because they are doctrinally or morally incompetent. The differentiation of roles for men and women in ministry is rooted not in any supposed incompetence but in God's created order for manhood and womanhood. Since little boys do not relate to their women teachers as men relate to women, the leadership dynamic ordained by God is not injured. (However, that dynamic would be injured if the pattern of our church staffing and teaching communicated that Bible teaching is only women's work and not the primary responsibility of the fathers and spiritual men of the church.)

31. Aren't you guilty of a selective literalism when you say some commands in a text are permanently valid and others, like "Don't wear braided hair" or "Do wear a head covering," are culturally conditioned and not absolute?

All of life and language is culturally conditioned. We share with all interpreters the challenge of discerning how biblical teaching should be applied today in a very different culture. In demonstrating the permanent validity of a command, we would try to show from its context that it has roots in the nature of God, the gospel, or creation as God ordered it. We would study these things as they are unfolded throughout Scripture.

In contrast, to show that the specific forms of some commands are limited to one kind of situation or culture, (1) we search for clues in the context that this is so; (2) we compare other Scriptures relating to the same subject to see if we are dealing with a limited application or with an abiding requirement; and (3) we try to show that the cultural specificity of the command is not rooted in the nature of God, the gospel, or the created order. In the context of Paul's and Peter's teaching about how men and women relate in the church and the home, there are instructions not only about submission and leadership but also about forms of feminine adornment. Here are the relevant verses in our literal translation:

> Likewise the women are to adorn themselves in respectable apparel with modesty and sensibleness, not in braids and gold or pearls or expensive clothing, but, as is fitting for women who profess godliness, through good works. (1 Tim. 2:9–10)

> Let not yours be the external adorning of braiding hair and putting on gold or wearing clothes, but the hidden person

of the heart by the imperishable (jewel) of a meek and quiet spirit, which is precious before God. (1 Pet. 3:3–5)

It would be wrong to say these commands are irrelevant today. One clear, abiding teaching in them is that *the focus* of effort at adornment should be on "good works" and on "the hidden person" rather than on the externals of clothing and hair and jewelry. Neither is there any reason to nullify the general command to be modest and sensible or the warning against ostentation. The only question is whether wearing braids, gold, and pearls is intrinsically sinful then and now.

There is one clear indication from the context that this was not the point. Peter says, "Let not yours be the external adorning of . . . wearing clothes." The Greek does not say "fine" clothes (NIV and RSV) but just "wearing clothes," that is, "the clothing you wear" (ESV) or "putting on dresses" (NASB). Now we know Peter is not condemning the use of clothes. He is condemning the *mis*use of clothes. This suggests, then, that the same thing could be said about gold and braids. The point is not to warn against something intrinsically evil but to warn against its misuse as an expression of self-exaltation or worldly-mindedness. Add to this that the commands concerning headship and submission are rooted in the created order (in 1 Tim. 2:13–14), while the specific forms of modesty are not. This is why we plead innocent of the charge of selective literalism.

32. But doesn't Paul argue for a head covering for women in worship by appealing to the created order in 1 Corinthians 11:13–15? Why is the head covering not binding today while the teaching concerning submission and headship is?

The key question here is whether Paul is saying that creation dictates a head covering or that creation dictates that we use culturally appropriate expressions of masculinity and femininity, which just happened to be a head covering for women in that setting. We think the latter is the case. The key verses are: "Judge for yourselves: is it proper for a wife to pray to God with her head uncovered? Does not nature itself teach you that if a man wears long hair it is a disgrace to him, but if a woman has long hair, it is her glory? For her hair is given to her for a covering" (1 Cor. 11:13–15).

How did nature teach that long hair dishonored a man and gave women a covering? Nature has not endowed women with more hair than men. In fact, if nature takes its course, men will have more hair than women because it will cover their face as well as their head. There must be another way that nature teaches on this subject! We believe custom and nature conspire in this pedagogy. On the one hand, *custom* dictates what hair arrangements are generally masculine or feminine. On the other hand, *nature* dictates that men feel ashamed when they wear symbols of femininity. We could feel the force of this by asking the men of our churches, "Does not nature teach you not to wear a dress to church?" The teaching of nature is the *natural* inclination of men and women to feel shame when they abandon the culturally established symbols of masculinity or femininity. Nature does not teach what the symbols should be.

When Paul says that a woman's hair "is given to her for a covering" (v. 15), he means that nature has given woman the hair and the inclination to follow prevailing customs of displaying her femininity, which in this case included letting her hair grow long and drawing it up into a covering for her head. So Paul's point in this passage is that the relationships of manhood and womanhood, which are rooted in the created order (1 Cor. 11:7–9), should find appropriate cultural expression in the worship service. Nature teaches this by giving men and women deep and differing inclinations about the use of masculine and feminine symbols.

33. How is it consistent to forbid the eldership to women in our churches and then send them out as missionaries to do things forbidden at home?

We stand in awe of the faith, love, courage, and dedication that have moved thousands of single and married women into missions. The story told by Ruth Tucker in *Guardians of the Great Commission: The Story of Women in Modern Missions*[15] is great. Our prayer is that it will inspire thousands more women—and men!—to give themselves to the great work of world evangelization.

Is this inconsistent of us? Is it true that we are sending women as missionaries to do "things forbidden" at home? If so, it is a remarkable fact that the vast majority of the women who have become missionaries over the centuries also endorsed the responsibility of men in leadership the way we do.[16] And the men who have most vigorously recruited and defended women for missions have done so not because they disagreed with our vision of manhood and womanhood but because they saw boundless work available in evangelism—some that women could do better than men.

For example, Hudson Taylor saw that when a Chinese catechist worked with a "missionary-sister" instead of a European male missionary, "the whole work of teaching and preaching and representing the mission to outsiders devolves upon him; he counts as the head of the mission, and must act independently."[17] The paradoxical missionary strength of being "weak" was recognized again and again. Mary Slessor, in an incredible display of strength, argued that she should be allowed to go alone to unexplored territory in Africa because "as a woman she would be less of a threat to native tribesmen than a male missionary would be, and therefore safer."[18]

Another example is A. J. Gordon, the Boston pastor, missionary, statesman, and founder (in 1889) of the Boston Missionary Training Institute that would later spawn both Gordon College and Gordon-Conwell Theological Seminary. He strongly promoted women in missions, appealing especially to the prophesying daughters of Acts 2:17. But for all his exuberance for the widest ministry of women in mission, he took a view of 1 Timothy 2:12 similar to ours:

> Admit, however, that the prohibition is against public teaching; what may it mean? To teach and to govern are the special functions of the presbyter. The teacher and the pastor, named in the gifts to the Church (Eph. 4:11), Alford considers to be the same; and the pastor is generally regarded as identical with the bishop. Now there is no instance in the New Testament of a woman being set over a church as bishop and teacher. The lack of such example would lead us to refrain from ordaining a woman as pastor of a Christian congregation. But if the Lord has fixed this limitation, we believe it to be grounded, not on her less favored position in the privileges of grace, but in the impediments to such service existing in nature itself.[19]

We admit that there are ambiguities in applying Paul's instructions about an established church to an emerging church. We admit that there are ambiguities in separating the Priscilla-type counsel from the official teaching role of 1 Timothy 2:12. We could imagine ourselves struggling for biblical and cultural faithfulness the way Hudson Taylor did in a letter to Miss Faulding in 1868:

> I do not know when I may be able to return, and it will not do for Church affairs to wait for me. You cannot take a Pastor's place in name, but you must help (Wang) Laedjun to act in matters of receiving and excluding as far as you can. You can speak privately to candidates, and can be present at Church meetings, and might even, through others, suggest questions to be asked of those desiring baptism. Then after the meeting you can talk privately with Laedjun about them, and suggest who you think he might receive next time they meet. Thus he may have the help he needs, and there will be nothing that any one could regard as unseemly.[20]

We do not wish to impede the great cause of world evangelization by quibbling over which of the hundreds of roles for missionaries might correspond so closely to the office of pastor/elder as to be inappropriate for a woman. It is apparent to us that women are fellow workers in the gospel and should strive side by side with men (Phil. 4:3; Rom. 16:3, 12). For the sake of finishing the Great Commission in our day, we are willing to risk some less-than-ideal role assignments.

We hope that we are not sending men or women to do things that are forbidden at home. We are not sending women to become the pastors or elders of churches. Neither have the vast majority of women evangelists and church planters sought this for themselves. We do not think it is forbidden for women to tell the gospel story and win men and women to Christ. We do not think God forbids women to work among the millions of lost women in the world, which according to Ruth Tucker "was the major justification of the Women's Missionary Movement."[21] Even if a woman held a more restrictive view than ours, the fact that over two-thirds of the world's precious lost people are women and children means that there are more opportunities in evangelism and teaching than could ever be exhausted.

Our passion is not to become the watchdogs of where women serve. Our passion is to join hands with all God's people, in God's way, to "declare his glory among the nations" (Ps. 96:3).

34. Do you deny women the right to use the gifts God has given them? Does not God's giving a spiritual gift imply that he endorses its use for the edification of the church?

Having a spiritual gift is not a warrant to use it however we please. John White is right when he writes, "Some people believe it to be impossible that the power of the Holy Spirit could have unholy consequences in an individual's life. But it can."[22] Spiritual gifts are not only given by the Holy Spirit, they are also regulated by the holy Scriptures. This is clear from 1 Corinthians, where people with the gift of tongues were told not to use it in public when there was no gift of interpretation and where prophets were told to stop prophesying when someone else had a revelation (1 Cor. 14:28–30). We do not deny women the right to use the gifts God has given them. If they have gifts of teaching or administration or evangelism, God does want them to use those gifts, and he will honor the commitment to use them within the guidelines given in Scripture.

35. If God has genuinely called a woman to be a pastor, then how can you say she should not be one?

We do not believe God genuinely calls women to be pastors. We say this not because we can read the private experience of anyone but because we believe private experience must always be assessed by the public criterion of God's Word, the Bible. If the Bible teaches that God wills for men alone to bear the primary teaching and governing responsibilities of the pastorate, then by implication the Bible also teaches that God does not call women to be pastors. The church has known from its earliest days that an individual's personal *sense* of divine leading is not *by itself* an adequate criterion for discerning God's call. Surely God sends chosen ministers (Rom. 10:15), but God also warns against those who thought they were called and were not: "I did not send them or charge them" (Jer. 23:32).

Probably what some earnest Christian women discern as a divine call to the pastorate is indeed a call to ministry but not to the pastorate. Very often the divine compulsion to serve comes upon Christians without the Holy Spirit specifying the precise avenue of service. At this point, we should look not only at our gifts but also at the teaching of Scripture regarding what is appropriate for us as men and women.

36. What is the meaning of authority when you talk about it in relation to the home and the church?

This question is crucial because the New Testament shows that the basic relationships of life fit together in terms of authority and compliance. For example, the relationship between parents and children works on the basis of the right of the parents to require obedience (Eph. 6:1–2). The civil government has authority to make laws that regulate the behavior of citizens (Rom. 13:1–7; Titus 3:1; 1 Pet. 2:13–17). Most social institutions have structures that give to some members the right to direct the actions of others. The military and the business sector come most readily to mind (Matt. 8:9; 1 Pet. 2:18–20).

The church, while made up of a priesthood of believers, is governed in the New Testament by servant-leaders whom the people are called to follow (1 Thess. 5:12; Heb. 13:7, 17; 1 Tim.

3:5; 5:17). In marriage the wife is called to submit to the sacrificial headship of her husband (Eph. 5:22–33; Col. 3:18–19; 1 Pet. 3:1–7). Finally, the source of all this authority is God's authority, which is absolute.

What becomes clear as soon as we try to give a definition to this authority is that its form changes from one relationship to another. We would define authority in general as the *right* (Matt. 8:9) and *power* (Mark 1:27; 1 Cor. 7:37) and *responsibility* (2 Cor. 10:8; 13:10) *to give direction to another*. This applies perfectly to God in all his relationships. But it applies in very different ways to various human relationships.

For example, with regard to the *power* to direct others, the state is invested with the sword (Rom. 13:4); parents are given the rod (Prov. 13:24); businesses can terminate an employee (Luke 16:2); and elders can, with the church, excommunicate (Matt. 18:17; 1 Cor. 5:1–8). Similarly, the extent of the *right* to direct others varies with each relationship. For example, parents have the right to be directly involved in the minutest details of their young children's lives, teaching them to hold their forks correctly and sit up straight. But the government and the church would not have such extensive rights.

For Christians, *right* and *power* recede and *responsibility* predominates. As Jesus said to his disciples, "You know that the rulers of the Gentiles lord it over them, and their great ones exercise authority over them. It shall not be so among you. But whoever would be great among you must be your servant" (Matt. 20:25–26). Authority becomes a burden to bear, not a right to assert. It is a sacred duty to discharge for the good of others. Excommunicating a church member is a painful last resort. A spanked child is enfolded in affection. Employers show mercy. But none of this abolishes authority structures; it rather transforms them as loving responsibility seeks to outrun rights and power.

The transformation of authority is most thorough in marriage. This is why we prefer to speak of authority in terms of leadership and headship. The Bible gives husbands no warrant to use physical power to bring wives into submission. When Ephesians 5:25–27 shows Christ bringing his bride toward holiness, it shows him suffering for her, not making her suffer for him. The husband's authority is a God-given burden to be carried in humility, not a natural right to flaunt with pride.

At least three things hinder a husband from using his authority (leadership!) to justify force: (1) the unique intimacy and union implied in the phrase "one flesh"—"no one ever hated his own flesh, but nourishes and cherishes it" (Eph. 5:29–31); (2) the special honor commanded in 1 Peter 3:7 for a husband to treat his wife as a joint heir of the grace of life; and (3) the aim to cultivate shared maturity in Christ, not childish dependence.

Thus, authority in general is the right, power, and responsibility to direct others. But the form and balance of these elements will vary in the different relationships of life according to the teachings of Scripture.

37. If a church embraces a congregational form of governance in which the congregation, and not the elders, is the highest authority under Christ and Scripture, should the women be allowed to vote?

Yes. Acts 15:22 says, "Then it seemed good to the apostles and the elders, with the whole church, to choose men from among them and send them to Antioch." This seems to be a biblical expression of the priesthood of all believers (1 Pet. 2:9; Rev. 1:6; 5:10; cf. Matt. 18:17). The reason we do not think this is inconsistent with 1 Timothy 2:12 is that the authority of the church is not the same as the authority of the individuals who make up the church. When we say the congregation has authority, we do not mean that each man and each woman has that authority. Therefore, gender, as a part of individual personhood, is not significantly in view in corporate congregational decisions.

38. In Romans 16:7, Paul wrote, "Greet Andronicus and Junia, my kinsmen and my fellow prisoners. They are well known to the apostles, and they were in Christ before me." Isn't Junia a woman? And wasn't she an apostle? And doesn't that mean that Paul was willing to acknowledge that a woman held a very authoritative position over men in the early church?

Let's take these three questions one at a time.

(1) Was Junia(s) a woman? We cannot know. The evidence is inconclusive, and some translations use Junia (a woman's name) and others Junias (a man's name). We did a complete search of all the Greek writings from Homer (ninth century BC?) into the fifth century AD now available digitally through the Thesaurus Linguae Graecae,[23] which contains 2,889 authors and 8,203 works. We searched for all forms of *Iounia-* so that we would pick up all the possible cases. (We did not search for the possible first declension masculine genitive *Iouniou*, which morphologically could come from a masculine *Iounias*, because there is no way to tell if *Iouniou* might come from a different man's name *Iounios* [ending in *-os* rather than *-as*], which would make all these genitive forms useless in establishing a masculine *Iounias* in Romans 16:7.)

Our computer search resulted in three instances besides the one in Romans 16:7:

a. Plutarch (ca. AD 50–ca. 120), in his *Life of Marcus Brutus*, wrote about the tension between Brutus and Cassius: "... though they were connected in their families, Cassius having married Junia, the sister of Brutus [*Iounia gar adelphe Broutou sunoikei Kassios*]."[24]
b. Epiphanius (AD 315–403), the bishop of Salamis in Cyprus, wrote an *Index of Disciples*, in which he includes this line: "Iounias, of whom Paul makes mention, became bishop of Apameia of Syria."[25] In Greek, the phrase "of whom" is a masculine relative pronoun (*hou*) and shows that Epiphanius thought Iounias was a man.
c. John Chrysostom (AD 347–407), in preaching on Romans 16:7, said in reference to Junia(s), "Oh! how great is the devotion of this woman, that she should be even counted worthy of the appellation of apostle!"[26]

What we may learn from these three uses is that Junia(s) was used as a woman's name in the time around the New Testament (Plutarch). The church fathers were evidently divided as to whether Paul was using Junia(s) that way, Epiphanius assuming it was masculine, Chrysostom assuming it was feminine. Perhaps somewhat more weight may be given to the statement by Epiphanius, since he appears to know more specific information about Junia(s) (that he became bishop of Apameia), while Chrysostom gives no more information than what he could deduce from Romans 16:7 (however, Epiphanius does give incorrect information about Prisca).[27]

Perhaps more significant than either of these, however, is a Latin quotation from Origen (d. AD 252) in the earliest extant commentary on Romans. He says that Paul refers to "Andronicus and Junias and Herodian, all of whom he calls relatives and fellow captives [*Andronicus, et Junias, et Herodion, quos omnes et cognatos suos, et concaptivos appellat*]."[28] The name Junias here is a Latin masculine singular nominative, implying—if this ancient translation is reliable—that Origen (who was one of the ancient world's most proficient scholars) thought Junia(s) was a man. Coupled with the quotation from Epiphanius, this quotation tips the scales of ancient evidence in support of this view.

Masculine names ending in *-as* are not unusual even in the New Testament: Andrew (*Andreas*, Matt. 10:2), Elijah (*Elias*, Matt. 11:14), Isaiah (*Esaias*, John 1:23), Zacharias (Luke 1:5). A. T. Robertson shows that numerous names ending in *-as* are shortened forms for clearly masculine forms.[29] The clearest example in the New Testament is Silas (Acts 15:22) from Silvanus (1 Thess. 1:1; 1 Pet. 5:12).

So there is no way to be dogmatic about what the form of the name signifies. It could be feminine or it could be masculine. Certainly no one should claim that Junia was a common woman's name in the Greek-speaking world, since we can identify only these three known examples in all of extant ancient Greek literature.[30] Moreover, the fact that Andronicus and Junia(s), like Prisca and Aquila (Rom. 16:3), are given as a pair does not demand that they be husband and wife, because in Romans 16:12 two women are greeted as a pair: "Greet those workers in the Lord, Tryphaena and Tryphosa." Andronicus and Junia(s) could be addressed as two men, since Tryphaena and Tryphosa are addressed as two women.

(2) Was Junia(s) an apostle? This seems highly unlikely. Grammatically, the phrase translated "of note among the apostles" in the RSV could mean that the apostles held Andronicus and Junia(s) in high regard (thus the ESV translation "well known to the apostles," which is the most likely translation according

to an extensive grammatical study[31]). Thus they would not be themselves apostles. On the other hand, since Andronicus and Junia(s) were Christians before Paul was, it may be that their long-standing ministry (reaching back before Paul's) is precisely what Paul has in mind when he says "well known to the apostles." They may indeed have been well known to the apostles before Paul was even converted.

(3) Did Junia(s) have a very authoritative position in the early church? Probably not. The word *apostle* is used for servants of Christ at different levels of authority in the New Testament. Revelation 21:14 refers to "the twelve apostles of the Lamb" (cf. Matt. 19:28; Acts 1:15–26). The twelve had a unique role in bearing witness to the resurrection of Jesus. Paul counted himself among the privileged group by insisting on having seen and been called by the risen Christ (1 Cor. 9:1–2; Gal. 1:1, 12). Very closely related with this unique inner ring were the missionary partners of Paul: Barnabas (Acts 14:14) and Silvanus and Timothy (1 Thess. 2:6), as well as James, the Lord's brother (Gal. 1:19), and perhaps others (1 Cor. 15:7).

Finally, the word *apostle* (Greek *apostolos*) is used in a broad sense as "messenger," for example, of Epaphroditus in Philippians 2:25 and of several "messengers of the churches" in 2 Corinthians 8:23. Therefore, even if Andronicus and Junia(s) were "apostles" in some sense of the word, they were probably in this third group serving in some kind of itinerant ministry. If Junia(s) is a woman, this would seem to put her in the same category with Priscilla, who with her husband seemed to do at least a little traveling with the apostle Paul (Acts 18:18). The ministry would be significant but not necessarily in the category of an authoritative governor of the churches like Paul (2 Cor. 10:8; 13:10).

39. Paul seems to base the primary responsibility of man to lead and teach on the fact that he was created first, before woman (1 Tim. 2:13). How is this a valid argument when the animals were created before man but don't have primary responsibility for leading him?

The contextual basis for this argument in the book of Genesis is the assumption throughout the book that the "firstborn" *in a human family* has the special right and responsibility of leadership in the family. When the Hebrews gave a special responsibility to the "firstborn," it never entered their minds that this responsibility would be nullified if the father happened to own cattle before he had sons. In other words, when Moses wrote this, he knew that the first readers would not lump animals and humans together as equal candidates for the responsibilities of the "firstborn." We shouldn't either.

Once this concern with the priority of animals is out of the way, the question that evangelical feminists must come to terms with is why God should choose to create man and woman sequentially. It won't do just to say, "Sequence doesn't *have* to mean leadership priority." The question is, "What does *this* sequence mean?" Why didn't God create them simultaneously out of the same dust? In the context of all the textual pointers assembled by Ray Ortlund Jr. in his chapter on Genesis 1–3 in *Recovering Biblical Manhood and Womanhood*, we think the most natural implication of God's decision to bring Adam onto the scene ahead of Eve is that Adam is called to bear the responsibility of headship. That fact is validated by the New Testament when Paul uses the fact that "Adam was formed first, then Eve" (1 Tim. 2:13), to draw a conclusion about male leadership in the church.

40. Isn't it true that the reason Paul did not permit women to teach was that women were not well educated in the first century? But that reason does not apply today. In fact, since women are as well educated as men today, shouldn't we allow both women and men to be pastors?

This objection does not match the data in the biblical text for at least three reasons: First, Paul does not give lack of education as a reason for saying that women are not "to teach or to exercise authority over a man" (1 Tim. 2:12) but rather points back to creation (1 Tim. 2:13–14). It is precarious to build an argument on a reason Paul did not give, instead of the reason he did give.

Second, formal training in Scripture was not required for leadership in the New Testament church—even several of the apostles did not have formal biblical training (Acts 4:13), while the skills of basic literacy, and therefore the ability to read and study Scripture, were available to men and women alike (note Acts 18:26; Rom. 16:1; 1 Tim. 2:11; Titus 2:3–4). The papyri show "widespread literacy" among Greek-speaking women in Egypt, and in Roman society, "many women were educated and witty."[32]

Third, if any woman in the New Testament church was well educated, it would have been Priscilla, yet Paul was writing 1 Timothy 2:12 to Ephesus (1 Tim. 1:3), the home church of Priscilla and Aquila. Beginning in AD 50, Paul had stayed at the home of Priscilla and Aquila in Corinth for eighteen months (Acts 18:2, 11); then they had gone with Paul to Ephesus in AD 51 (Acts 18:18–19, 21). Even by that time, Priscilla knew Scripture well enough to help instruct Apollos (Acts 18:26). Then she had probably learned from Paul himself for another three years while he stayed at Ephesus teaching "the whole counsel of God" (Acts 20:27; cf. v. 31; 1 Cor. 16:19), and no doubt many other women in Ephesus followed her example and also learned from Paul. Aquila and Priscilla had gone to Rome sometime later (Rom. 16:3), about AD 58, but apparently had returned, for they were in Ephesus again at the end of Paul's life (2 Tim. 4:19), about AD 67. Therefore, it is likely that they were back in Ephesus in AD 65 around the time Paul wrote 1 Timothy (persecution of Christians began in Rome in AD 64). Yet not even well-educated Priscilla, nor any other well-educated women in Ephesus, were allowed to teach men in the public assembly of the church: writing to Ephesus, Paul said, "I do not permit a woman to teach or to exercise authority over a man" (1 Tim. 2:12). The reason was not lack of education, but God's creation order.

41. Why do you bring up homosexuality when discussing male and female role distinctions in the home and the church (as in question 1)? Most evangelical feminists are just as opposed as you are to the practice of homosexuality.

We bring up homosexuality because we believe that by minimizing the differences in sexual roles, feminists contribute to the confusion of sexual identity that, especially in the second and third generations, gives rise to more homosexuality in society. Some evangelicals who once disapproved of homosexuality have been carried by their feminist arguments to the approval of faithful homosexual alliances. For example, Gerald Sheppard, a professor of Old Testament Literature at Emmanuel College in the University of Toronto, was nurtured in a conservative evangelical tradition and attended an evangelical seminary. In recent years he has argued for the ordination of women to the pastorate. He has also moved on to say, "On a much more controversial matter, the presence of gay and lesbian Christians and ministers in our churches is for me a similar issue. . . . I believe that the Gospel—as Evangelicals Concerned recognizes—should lead us at least to an affirmation of gay and lesbian partnerships ruled by a biblical ethic analogous to that offered for heterosexual relationships."[33]

Another example is Karen J. Torjesen, who argues that removing hierarchy in sexual relations will probably mean that the primacy of heterosexual marriage will have to go:

> It would appear that, in Paul, issues of sexuality are theologically related to hierarchy, and therefore the issues of biblical feminism and lesbianism are irrefutably intertwined. We need to grapple with the possibility that our conflicts over the appropriate use of human sexuality may rather be conflicts rooted in a need to legitimate the traditional social structure which assigns men and women specific and unequal positions. Could it be that the continued affirmation of the primacy of heterosexual marriage is possibly also the affirmation of the necessity for the sexes to remain in a hierarchically structured relationship? Is the threat to the "sanctity of marriage" really a threat to hierarchy? Is that what makes same-sex relations so threatening, so frightening?[34]

The Evangelical Women's Caucus was split in 1986 over whether there should be "recognition of the presence of the lesbian minority in EWCI."[35] We are glad that many evangelical women distanced themselves from the endorsement of lesbianism. But what is significant is how many evangelical feminists considered the endorsement "a step of maturity within the organization" (e.g., Nancy Hardesty and Virginia Mollenkott). In other words, they view the movement away from role distinctions grounded in the natural created order as leading inevitably to the overthrow of normative heterosexuality. It seems to us that the evangelical feminists who do not embrace homosexuality will be increasingly hard put to escape this logic.

Paul Jewett, too, seems to illustrate a move from biblical feminism toward endorsing certain expressions of homosexuality. In his defense of equal roles for men and women in *Man as Male and Female* in 1975, he said that he was uncertain "what it means to be a man in distinction to a woman or a woman in distinction to a man."[36] That seemed to us to bode ill for preserving the primacy of heterosexuality. In 1983, he reviewed the historical defense of homosexuality by John Boswell, who argued that Paul's meaning in Romans 1:26–27 was that the only thing condemned was homosexual behavior by heterosexuals, not by homosexuals who acted according to their "nature." Jewett rejected this interpretation with the words, "For [Paul] the 'nature' against which a homosexual acts is not simply his individual nature, but the generic human nature in which he shares as an individual."[37]

This was gratifying, but it seemed strange again to us that he would say homosexual behavior is a sin against "generic *human* nature" rather than *masculine* or *feminine* nature. Then, in 1985, Jewett seemed to give away the biblical case for heterosexuality in a review of Robin Scroggs's book, *The New Testament and Homosexuality*. Scroggs argued that the passages that relate to homosexual behavior in the New Testament "are irrelevant and provide no help in the heated debate today" because they refer not to homosexual "inversion," which is a natural orientation, but to homosexual "perversion."[38] Jewett responded, "If this is the meaning of the original sources—and the scholarship is competent, the argument is careful and, therefore, the conclusion is rather convincing—then what the New Testament is against is something significantly different from a homosexual orientation which some people have from their earliest days."[39] (More recently, other prominent evangelical feminists have voiced their endorsement of committed homosexual relationships, including Jim Wallis, Anthony Campolo, and David Neff.)[40]

But even evangelical feminists who continue to agree with us that Scripture views homosexual conduct as sinful face the very real danger of imparting gender role confusion to their children. How can a firm and loving affirmation of a son's masculinity or a daughter's femininity be cultivated in an atmosphere where role differences between masculinity and femininity are constantly denied or minimized? If the only significant role differentiation is based on competency and has no root in nature, what will parents do to shape the sexual identity of their children? If they say that they will do nothing, common sense and many psychological studies tell us that the children will be confused about who they are and will therefore be far more likely to develop a homosexual orientation.

To us, it is increasingly and painfully clear that biblical feminism is an unwitting partner in unraveling the fabric of the complementary manhood and womanhood that provide the foundation not only for biblical marriage and biblical church order but also for heterosexuality itself.

42. How do you know that your interpretation of Scripture is not influenced more by your background and culture than by what the authors of Scripture actually intended?

We are keenly aware of our fallibility. We feel the forces of culture, tradition, and personal inclination, as well as the deceitful darts of the Devil. We have our personal predispositions and have no doubt been influenced by all the genetic and environmental constraints of our past and present, and we hope we are not above correction. But we take heart that some measure of freedom from falsehood is possible, because the Bible encourages us not to be conformed to this age but to be transformed by the renewing of our minds (Rom. 12:1–2).

Whether feminists are more influenced by the immense cultural pressure of contemporary egalitarian assumptions or we are more influenced by centuries of patriarchalism and by our own masculine drives is hard to say. It does little good for us to impugn each other on the basis of these partially subconscious influences. It is clear from the literature that we all have our suspicions.

Nonetheless, our confidence in the convictions we hold is based on five facets of our pursuit of truth: (1) we regularly search our motives and seek to empty ourselves of all that would tarnish a true perception of reality; (2) we pray that God would give us humility, teachability, wisdom, insight, fairness, and honesty; (3) we make every effort to submit our minds to the unbending and unchanging grammatical and historical reality of the biblical texts in Greek and Hebrew, using the best methods of study available to get as close as possible to the intentions of the biblical writers; (4) we compare our conclusions with the history of exegesis to reveal any chronological snobbery or cultural myopia; and (5) we test our conclusions in the real world of contemporary ministry and look for resonance from mature and godly people. In humble confidence that we are handling the Scriptures with care, we lay our vision now before the public for all to see and debate in public forum.

43. Why is it acceptable to sing hymns written by women and recommend books written by women but not to permit them to say the same things audibly?

We do not say that a woman cannot say the same things audibly. When Paul says, "be filled with the Spirit, addressing one another in psalms and hymns and spiritual songs" (Eph. 5:18–19), we imagine women in the congregation reciting or singing for the church what God has given them (perhaps, in some cases, as a kind of "prophecy," like that mentioned in 1 Cor. 11:5). Moreover, we rejoice in the inevitable fact that men as well as women will learn and be built up and encouraged by this poetic ministry.

We have not, of course, ruled out either small or worldwide ministries of women teaching other women. The issue for us is whether a woman should function as part of the primary teaching leadership (i.e., eldership) in a fellowship of women and men, and it seems to us that publicly teaching a congregation from the Scriptures does just that. By contrast, when an individual person reads a book written by a woman (even a Bible commentary that "teaches" Scripture), the dynamic is closer to that of the private conversation among Apollos, Priscilla, and Aquila in Acts 18:26 (see question 20) than it is to the public teaching of a congregation that Paul prohibits in 1 Timothy 2:12. We also recognize the ambiguities involved in making wise and thoughtful distinctions between the kinds of public speaking that are appropriate and inappropriate. Our expectation is not that we will all arrive at exactly the same sense of where to draw these lines but that we might come to affirm together the underlying principles. Obedient, contemporary application of ethical teachings (e.g., the teachings of Jesus on poverty and wealth, anger and forgiveness, justice and nonretaliation) has always been laden with difficult choices.

44. Isn't giving women access to all offices and roles a simple matter of justice that even our society recognizes?

We are aware that the question is increasingly being posed in terms of justice. For example, Nicholas Wolterstorff says, "The question that women in the church are raising is a question of justice. . . . Women are not asking for handouts of charity from us men. They are asking that in the Church—in the Church of all places—they receive their due. They are asking why gender is relevant for assigning tasks and roles and offices and responsibilities and opportunities in the Church."[41]

Clearly, we think gender is relevant for determining the justice of roles and responsibilities. Perhaps the best way to show why is to cite an article from the *Minneapolis Star-Tribune*.[42] The author, Thomas B. Stoddard, told the story of two lesbians, Karen Thompson and Sharon Kowalski, of Minnesota. "Thompson and Kowalski are spouses in every respect," he writes, "except the legal." (At the time Stoddard wrote, every jurisdiction in the United States refused to permit two individuals of the same sex to marry.) "They exchanged vows and rings; they lived together until Nov. 13, 1983—when Kowalski was severely injured when her car was struck by a drunk driver. She lost the capacity to walk or to speak more than several words at a time, and needed constant care. Thompson sought a court ruling granting her guardianship over her partner, but Kowalski's parents opposed the petition and obtained sole guardianship. They moved Kowalski to a nursing home three hundred miles away from Thompson and forbade all visits."

Stoddard uses this story to illustrate the painful effects of the "monstrous *injustice*" of "depriving millions of gay American adults the marriages of their choice." His argument is that gay marriages "create families and promote social stability. In an increasingly loveless world, those who wish to commit themselves to a relationship founded upon devotion should be encouraged, not scorned. Government has no legitimate interest in how that love is expressed."

This raises a very fundamental question: How does natural existence relate to moral duty? Or what moral constraints does our birth as male or female put upon us? Does God intend that maleness should confront men with any moral demands that are different from the moral demands with which femaleness confronts women?

The answer is not simple. On the one hand we would cry, no! The Ten Commandments apply equally to men and women with no distinctions. But on the other hand, most of us would also cry, yes! It is a sin for a man to marry a man but not for a woman to marry a man (Rom. 1:26–27). If this is so, we *cannot* say that what we are by *nature* (gender) plays no role in determining our moral duty in relation to other people.

When a man stands before a woman, the moral duty that confronts him is not identical with his duty when he stands before a man. God has ordained that the natural and moral worlds intersect at, among other places, the point of our sexuality.

Until the recent emergence of gay pride, scarcely anyone would have accused God of discriminating against women by giving only men the right to marry women. Historically, it did not seem unjust that *solely* on the basis of gender God would exclude half the human race as lawful spouses for women. It seemed "fitting" and "natural" and "right" (dare we say, "just") that a large array of marital feelings and actions should be denied to women and men in their relations to half the human race.

The reason there was no worldwide revolt against this enormous limitation of our freedom in previous generations was probably that it squared with what most of us felt was appropriate and desirable anyway. In his mercy God had not allowed the inner voice of nature to be so distorted as to leave the world with no sense of moral fitness in this affair.

Evangelical feminists might say that gender is relevant in defining justice in regard to *marriage* because nature teaches by the *anatomy* and *physiology* of man and woman what is just and right. But we ask, is that really the only basis in nature for marriage? Are we left only with anatomical differences as the ground of heterosexual marriage? One of the theses of this book is that the natural fitness of man and woman for each other in marriage is rooted in something more than anatomy. There is a profound female or male personhood portrayed in our differing bodies. As Emil Brunner once put it:

> Our sexuality penetrates to the deepest metaphysical ground of our personality. As a result, the physical differences between the man and the woman are a parable of psychical and spiritual differences of a more ultimate nature.[43]

Or as Otto Piper said, "Though [the difference between the sexes] has a sexual basis, its actuality covers all aspects of personal life."[44]

Perhaps, if evangelical feminists, who do not endorse the justice of homosexual marriages, would agree that the basis of their position is not mere anatomy but also the deeper differences of manhood and womanhood, then they could at least understand why we are hesitant to jettison such deeper differences when thinking through the nature of justice in other relational issues besides who may marry whom. The point of our book is that Scripture and nature teach that personal manhood and womanhood are indeed relevant in deciding not only whom to marry but also who gives primary leadership in the relationship.

45. Isn't it true that God is called our "helper" numerous times in the Bible with the same word used to describe Eve when she was called a "helper" suitable for man? Doesn't that rule out any notion of a uniquely submissive role for her, or even make her more authoritative than the man?

It is true that God is often called our "helper," but the word itself does not imply anything about rank or authority. The context must decide whether Eve is to "help" as a strong person who aids a weaker one or as one who assists a loving leader. The context makes it very unlikely that "helper" should be read on the analogy of God's help, because in Genesis 2:19–20 Adam first seeks his "helper" among the animals. But the animals will not do, because they are not "fit for him." So God makes the woman "from the man" (v. 22). Now there is a being who is "fit for him," sharing his human nature, equal to him in godlike personhood. She is infinitely different from an animal, and God highlights her value to man by showing how no animal can fill her role. Yet in passing through "helpful" animals to woman, God teaches us that the woman is a man's "helper" in the sense of a loyal and suitable assistant in the life of the garden.

The question wrongly assumes that because a word (like *helper*) has certain connotations ("godlikeness") in some places, it must have them in every place. This would be like saying that because God is described as one who "works" for us, therefore no human who "works" is responsible to his boss, since the word couldn't have that meaning when used of God.

46. Literally, 1 Corinthians 7:3–5 says, "The husband should give to his wife her conjugal rights, and likewise the wife to her husband. For the wife does not have authority over her own body, but the husband does. Likewise the husband does not

have authority over his own body, but the wife does. Do not deprive one another, except perhaps by agreement for a limited time, that you may devote yourselves to prayer." Doesn't this show that unilateral authority from the husband is wrong?

Yes. But let's broaden our answer to get the most from this text and guard it from misuse.

This text could be terribly misused by unloving men who take it as a license for thoughtless sexual demands or even lewd and humiliating erotic activity. One can imagine a man's sarcastic jab: "The Bible says that you do not have authority over your body, but I do. And it says, you *owe* me what I want." The reason we say this would be a *misuse* is because the text also gives to the wife the authority to say, "The Bible says that you do not have authority over your body, but I do, and I tell you that I do not want you to use your body to do that to me." Another reason we know this would be a misuse is that Paul says decisions in this sensitive area should be made "by agreement" (v. 5).

This text is not a license for sexual exploitation. It is an application to the sexual life of the command, "Outdo one another in showing honor" (Rom. 12:10). Or, "In humility count others more significant than yourselves" (Phil. 2:3). Or, "Only do not use your freedom as an opportunity for the flesh, but through love serve one another" (Gal. 5:13). The focus is not on what we have a right to take but on the debt we have to pay. Paul does not say, "Take what you want." He says, "Do not deprive each other." In other words, when it lies within your power to meet your spouse's needs, do it.

There is a wonderful mutuality and reciprocity running through the 1 Corinthians text from verse 2 to verse 5. Neither husband nor wife is given more rights over the body of the other. And when some suspension of sexual activity is contemplated,

Paul repudiates unilateral decision making by the wife or the husband: "Do not deprive one another, except perhaps by *agreement* for a limited time" (v. 5).

What are the implications of this text for the leadership of the husband? Do the call for mutual yielding to sexual need and the renunciation of unilateral planning nullify the husband's responsibility for general leadership in the marriage? We don't think so. But this text definitely shapes that leadership and gives added biblical guidance for how to work it out. It makes clear that his leadership will not involve selfish, unilateral choices. He will always strive for the ideal of agreement. He will take into account the truth that her sexual needs and desires carry the same weight as his own in developing the pattern of their intimacy.

This text makes crystal clear that leadership is not synonymous with having to get one's way. This text is also one of the main reasons we prefer to use the term *leadership* rather than *authority* for the man's special responsibility (see question 36). Texts like 1 Corinthians 7 transform the concept of *authority* so deeply as to make the word, with its authoritarian connotations, easily misunderstood. The difference between us and the evangelical feminists is that they think the concept disappears into mutuality, while we think the concept is shaped by mutuality.

47. If you believe that role distinctions for men and women in the home and the church are rooted in God's created order, why are you not as insistent about applying the rules everywhere in secular life as you are in the home and the church?

As we move out from the church and the home, we move further from what is fairly clear and explicit to what is more ambiguous and inferential, and we move from roles that are explicitly taught in Scripture to roles about which Scripture does not give explicit commands. Therefore, in such matters, our emphasis moves more and more away from specific role recommendations (like the ones made in Scripture) and instead focuses on the realization of male and female personhood through the more subjective dimensions of relationship like demeanor, bearing, attitudes, courtesies, initiatives, and numerous spoken and unspoken expectations.

We believe the Bible makes clear that men should take primary responsibility for leadership in the home and that, in the church, the primary teaching and governing leadership should be given by spiritual men. We take this to be a biblical expression of the goodness and the wisdom of God concerning the nature of leadership in these roles and the nature of manhood and womanhood. That is, rather than leaving us to judge for ourselves whether mature manhood and womanhood would be preserved and enhanced through the primary leadership of men or women in these spheres, God was explicit about what would be good for us. However, when it comes to all the thousands of occupations and professions, with their endlessly varied structures of management, God has chosen not to be specific about which roles men and women should fill.

Therefore, we are not as sure in this wider sphere which roles can be carried out by men or women in ways that honor the unique worth of male and female personhood. We do not want to make restrictions where Scripture itself does not make restrictions. For this reason we focus (with some exceptions) on *how* these roles are carried out rather than which ones are appropriate.[45]

48. How can a single Christian woman enter into the mystery of Christ and the church if she never experiences marriage?

Elisabeth Elliot has given an answer to this that we prefer to quote rather than try (in vain) to improve:

> The gift of virginity, given to every one to offer back to God for His use, is a priceless and irreplaceable gift. It can be offered in the pure sacrifice of marriage, or it can be offered in the sacrifice of a life's celibacy. Does this sound just too, too high and holy? But think for a moment—because the virgin has never known a man, she is free to concern herself wholly with the Lord's affairs, as Paul said in 1 Corinthians 7, "and her aim in life is to make herself holy, in body and spirit." She keeps her heart as the Bride of Christ in a very special sense, and offers to the Heavenly Bridegroom alone all that she is and has. When she gives herself willingly to Him in love she has no need to justify herself to the world or to Christians who plague her with questions and suggestions. In a way not open to the married woman her daily "living sacrifice" is a powerful and humble witness, radiating love. I believe she may enter into the "mystery" more deeply than the rest of us.[46]

49. Since many leading evangelical scholars disagree on the questions of manhood and womanhood, how can any layperson even hope to come to a clear conviction on these questions?

Two of the concerns that prompted us to form the Council on Biblical Manhood and Womanhood were (1) "the increasing prevalence and acceptance of hermeneutical oddities devised to reinterpret apparently plain meanings of Biblical texts," and (2) "the consequent threat to Biblical authority as the clarity of Scripture is jeopardized and the accessibility of its meaning to ordinary people is withdrawn into the restricted realm of technical ingenuity."[47]

Serious students of the Bible must walk a fine line between two dangers. On the one side is the oversimplification of the process of interpretation that neglects the disciplines of historical and grammatical study. On the other side is the temptation to pull rank on laypeople and emphasize inaccessible data and complicated contextual problems so much that they despair of confident understanding. We realize that there are "some things in [Paul's letters] that are hard to understand, which the ignorant and unstable twist to their own destruction, as they do the other Scriptures" (2 Pet. 3:16). This recognition will guard us from overstating the simplicity of Scripture.

But we believe the emphasis should fall on the usefulness of all Scripture. "All Scripture is breathed out by God and profitable for teaching, for reproof, for correction, and for training in righteousness, that the man of God may be complete, equipped for every good work" (2 Tim. 3:16–17). We do not want to discourage any serious layperson with the thought that the usefulness of Scripture is out of his or her reach. We also want to stress that under divine inspiration, the apostle Paul was committed to clarity and forthrightness in his writing: "We have renounced disgraceful, underhanded ways. We refuse to practice cunning or to tamper with God's word, but by the open statement of the truth we would commend ourselves to everyone's conscience in the sight of God" (2 Cor. 4:2).

We would also encourage laypeople to view controversies over important issues not only as evidence of our sin and ignorance but also as evidence that truth matters, that it is worth striving for, and that harmful error is not carrying the day unopposed. Paul said to the Corinthians, "When you come together as a church, I hear that there are divisions among you. And I believe it in part, for there must be factions among you in order that those who are genuine among you may be recognized" (1 Cor. 11:18–19). We are far from doubting the genuine Christian standing of evangelical feminists. The point here is that controversy is necessary where truth matters and serious error is spreading. Laypeople should therefore take heart that the battle for truth is being fought. They should realize that many of the plain things they virtually take for granted in their faith today were once hotly disputed and were preserved for them through controversy.

On this issue of manhood and womanhood, we encourage laypeople to consider the arguments available to them, to think for themselves, to saturate themselves in Scripture, and to pray earnestly for what Paul promised in Philippians 3:15: "If in anything you think otherwise, *God will reveal that also to you.*" For more guidance in this process we refer you to what is said above in question 42 and to *Recovering Biblical Manhood and Womanhood*, chapter 26, pages 418–20, where we discuss the guidance of the Spirit in this matter.

50. If a group of texts is hotly disputed, wouldn't it be a good principle of interpretation not to allow them any significant influence over our view of manhood and womanhood? Similarly, since there is significant disagreement in the church over the issue of men's and women's roles, should we not view this as having a very low level of importance in defining denominational, institutional, and congregational standards of belief and practice?

As to setting aside disputed texts, this would be a bad principle of interpretation. First, almost every text about precious and important things is disputed in some way and by some Christians. Never in history has there been so much pluralism under the banner of the Bible as there is today. Second, imagine what it would mean if we took no stand on things because they were disputed. It would make Satan's aim to mislead us much easier. He would not have to overthrow the truth of biblical texts; he would only have to create enough confusion that we would put the important ones aside. Third, leaving Satan out for a moment, we are all biased and would very likely use this principle of interpretation to justify neglecting the texts that do not suit our bias while insisting that the ones that suit our bias are crystal clear.

This, it seems to us, is the Achilles' heel of the hermeneutical approach adopted by Gretchen Gaebelein Hull in her book *Equal to Serve*. She takes one set of texts to be clear and undisputed, then takes another set to be obscure and disputed, and then says that the obscure ones should not have a crucial say in shaping our understanding of the issue. Specifically, she takes Genesis 1–2, the examples of female leaders (e.g., Deborah, Huldah, Miriam, Abigail, etc.), the ministry of Jesus to women, the examples of ministering women in the New Testament, plus texts on the redemptive equality of women (like 2 Cor. 5:14–21), and she infers that they *clearly* teach that male headship, in any distinctive form, is wrong. But all the texts in the New Testament that seem to teach an abiding role distinction for women and men she says are obscure and cannot make their contribution to the shape of our vision of manhood and womanhood. In the following lines she illustrates her method vis-à-vis the love of God and then applies it to the issue at hand:

> Everything I know about God indicates that He is indeed love, so loving that He came Himself to die for me. Therefore I put to one side passages like the Imprecatory Psalms or the Canaanite Wars that I do not understand. But I do not throw out the known truth "God is love," simply because some passages about the nature of God puzzle me.

> So we should also treat the three "hard passages" about women [1 Corinthians 11:2–16; 14:33b–36; 1 Timothy 2:8–15], which we find in the New Testament and which appear to place specific restrictions on women only. To these we could add Colossians 3:18; Ephesians 5:22–24; and 1 Peter 3:1–6. . . . Therefore we may legitimately put these Scripture portions aside for the very reason that they remain "hard passages"—hard exegetically, hard hermeneutically, and hard theologically.[48]

In this way, very crucial texts are silenced by the governing theme of "sex-blind" egalitarianism, which is itself built on disputed texts. This illustrates the danger of a principle that says, if a text is disputed, don't use it. Our procedure should be rather to continue to read Scripture carefully and prayerfully, seeking a position that dismisses no texts but interprets all the relevant texts of Scripture in a coherent way. And then we are to obey that consistent teaching.

Now as to the matter of "significant disagreement in the church over the issues of men's and women's roles," we need to realize first that significant disagreement in the church does not mean that the issue at stake is unimportant. The history of doctrinal controversy teaches us that very important matters (as well as less important ones) have been the subject of serious controversy. In fact, the length and intensity of a controversy may be evidence of the issue's importance, not of its unimportance.

If we examine the lists of expected standards for most denominations, institutions, and congregations, we discover that some articles (perhaps most) were included because a controversy swirled around that truth and a stand needed to be taken for the health of the church and the cause of Christ's kingdom. This means that many precious truths may not be included in our doctrinal and ethical standards at any given point in history because they were simply taken for granted in the absence of controversy. For example, until recently, standards have not generally included explicit statements on homosexual practice or certain kinds of drug abuse.

Most Christian denominations, institutions, and congregations have long taken for granted the primary responsibility of a husband to lead his family and the primary responsibility of spiritual men to lead the church. Therefore, these biblical truths have not received explicit statement in the formal standards. Their absence is a sign *not* of their relative unimportance but (almost the exact opposite) of their deep, pervasive, and longstanding worth in the Christian community. Thus we have the anomalous situation today that institutional affirmations of faith and practice include some things far less important, we believe, than what is at stake in this issue. For example, we would say that the issues of infant versus believer's baptism, of premillennialism, and of presbyterian, congregational, or episcopal polity are less threatening to the health and mission of the church than questions of gender roles.

Moreover, not to take a stand on this issue in our culture is to take a very decisive stand because of the relentless pressure for change that feminists are applying on many sides. Public advocacy on this issue results in so much criticism that many Christian leaders strive to avoid it. But there is no avoiding it. It is a massive issue that goes to the depths of who we are as persons and therefore touches all of life. Our counsel here is not to set out a specific strategy to preserve God's gift of sexual complementarity. Rather, we simply plead for Christian leaders to awaken to the importance of what is at stake and seek wisdom from above for how to act for the good of the church and the glory of God.

Appendix

The Danvers Statement on Biblical Manhood and Womanhood

In December 1987, the newly formed Council on Biblical Manhood and Womanhood met in Danvers, Massachusetts, and wrote the *Danvers Statement*. The full text of that statement follows:

Rationale

We have been moved in our purpose by the following contemporary developments which we observe with deep concern:

1. The widespread uncertainty and confusion in our culture regarding the complementary differences between masculinity and femininity;
2. the tragic effects of this confusion in unraveling the fabric of marriage woven by God out of the beautiful and diverse strands of manhood and womanhood;
3. the increasing promotion given to feminist egalitarianism with accompanying distortions or neglect of the glad harmony portrayed in Scripture between the loving, humble

leadership of redeemed husbands and the intelligent, willing support of that leadership of redeemed wives;

4. the widespread ambivalence regarding the values of motherhood, vocational homemaking, and the many ministries historically performed by women;
5. the growing claims of legitimacy for sexual relationships which have Biblically and historically been considered illicit or perverse, and the increase in pornographic portrayal of human sexuality;
6. the upsurge of physical and emotional abuse in the family;
7. the emergence of roles for men and women in church leadership that do not conform to Biblical teaching but backfire in the crippling of Biblically faithful witness;
8. the increasing prevalence and acceptance of hermeneutical oddities devised to reinterpret apparently plain meanings of Biblical texts;
9. the consequent threat to Biblical authority as the clarity of Scripture is jeopardized and the accessibility of its meaning to ordinary people is withdrawn into the restricted realm of technical ingenuity;
10. and behind all this the apparent accommodation of some with the church to the spirit of the age at the expense of winsome, radical Biblical authenticity which in the power of the Holy Spirit may reform rather than reflect our ailing culture.

Affirmations

Based on our understanding of Biblical teachings, we affirm the following:

1. Both Adam and Eve were created in God's image, equal before God as persons and distinct in their manhood and womanhood (Gen 1:26–27; 2:18).

2. Distinctions in masculine and feminine roles are ordained by God as part of the created order, and should find an echo in every human heart (Gen 2:18, 21–24; 1 Cor 11:7–9; 1 Tim 2:12–14).
3. Adam's headship in marriage was established by God before the Fall, and was not a result of sin (Gen 2:16–18, 21–24; 3:1–13; 1 Cor 11:7–9).
4. The Fall introduced distortions into the relationships between men and women (Gen 3:1–7, 12, 16).
   - In the home, the husband's loving, humble headship tends to be replaced by domination or passivity; the wife's intelligent, willing submission tends to be replaced by usurpation or servility.
   - In the church, sin inclines men toward a worldly love of power or an abdication of spiritual responsibility, and inclines women to resist limitations on their roles or to neglect the use of their gifts in appropriate ministries.
5. The Old Testament, as well as the New Testament, manifests the equally high value and dignity which God attached to the roles of both men and women (Gen 1:26–27; 2:18; Gal 3:28). Both Old and New Testament also affirm the principle of male headship in the family and in the covenant community (Gen 2:18; Eph 5:21–33; Col 3:18–19; 1 Tim 2:11–15).
6. Redemption in Christ aims at removing the distortions introduced by the curse.
   - In the family, husbands should forsake harsh or selfish leadership and grow in love and care for their wives; wives should forsake resistance to their husbands' authority and grow in willing, joyful submission to their husbands' leadership (Eph 5:21–33; Col 3:18–19; Tit 2:3–5; 1 Pet 3:1–7).

- In the church, redemption in Christ gives men and women an equal share in the blessings of salvation; nevertheless, some governing and teaching roles within the church are restricted to men (Gal 3:28; 1 Cor 11:2–16; 1 Tim 2:11–15).

7. In all of life Christ is the supreme authority and guide for men and women, so that no earthly submission—domestic, religious or civil—ever implies a mandate to follow a human authority into sin (Dan 3:10–18; Acts 4:19–20; 5:27–29; 1 Pet 3:1–2).
8. In both men and women a heartfelt sense of call to ministry should never be used to set aside Biblical criteria for particular ministries (1 Tim 2:11–15; 3:1–13; Tit 1:5–9). Rather, Biblical teaching should remain the authority for testing our subjective discernment of God's will.
9. With half the world's population outside the reach of indigenous evangelism; with countless other lost people in those societies that have heard the gospel; with the stresses and miseries of sickness, malnutrition, homelessness, illiteracy, ignorance, aging, addiction, crime, incarceration, neuroses, and loneliness, no man or woman who feels a passion from God to make His grace known in word and deed need ever live without a fulfilling ministry for the glory of Christ and the good of this fallen world (1 Cor 12:7–21).
10. We are convinced that a denial or neglect of these principles will lead to increasingly destructive consequences in our families, our churches, and the culture at large.

We grant permission and encourage interested persons to use, reproduce, and distribute the *Danvers Statement*. For copies of the *Danvers Statement*, please visit our website: www.cbmw.org.

Notes

Introduction: Complementarity

1. Larry Crabb, *Men and Women, Enjoying the Difference* (Grand Rapids, MI: Zondervan, 1991), 174.
2. Charles W. Colson, "What Can Gender Blending Render?" *World* 5 (March 2, 1991): 11.
3. See also Wayne Grudem, *Evangelical Feminism and Biblical Truth: An Analysis of Over 100 Disputed Questions* (Sisters, OR: Multnomah, 2004; Wheaton, IL: Crossway, 2012); Wayne Grudem, *Evangelical Feminism: A New Path to Liberalism?* (Wheaton, IL: Crossway, 2006); and John Piper, *What's the Difference? Manhood and Womanhood Defined According to the Bible* (Wheaton, IL: Crossway, 1990).

50 Crucial Questions

1. "Mission & Vision," The Council on Biblical Manhood and Womanhood, accessed June 3, 2015, http://cbmw.org/mission-vision/.
2. John Piper and Wayne Grudem, eds., *Recovering Biblical Manhood and Womanhood: A Response to Evangelical Feminism* (Wheaton, IL: Crossway, 1991). This title was also rereleased in 2006 with a new preface by J. Ligon Duncan and Randy Stinson.
3. This includes patterns stemming from negligence and abuses by both husband and wife. As the *Danvers Statement* says, "In the home, the husband's loving, humble headship tends to be replaced by domination or passivity; the wife's intelligent, willing submission tends to be replaced by usurpation or servility." Our aim is to work from both sides to promote what Christ really intended his relationship to the church to look like.
4. Two views of Eph. 5:21 are consistent with the position of this book. One view is that the verse teaches "mutual submission" of all Christians to one another and that vv. 22–33 teach specific kinds of submission. This interpretation is consistent with the overall ethical teaching of Scripture, for it is

correct to say that we should "submit to one another" in the sense of acting in a loving, considerate, self-giving way toward one another.

However, within the broad range of agreement among complementarians (as expressed, for example, in our larger edited volume, *Recovering Biblical Manhood and Womanhood*), there is room for another interpretation of Eph. 5:21, namely, that it does not teach "mutual submission" at all but rather teaches that we should all be subject to those whom God has put in authority over us—such as husbands, parents, or employers (5:22; 6:1, 5). In this way, Eph. 5:21 would be paraphrased, "being subject to one another (that is, *to some others*) in the fear of Christ."

The primary argument for this alternative view is the Greek word *hypotasso* ("to submit") itself. Although many people have claimed that the word can mean "be thoughtful and considerate; act in love" (toward another), it is doubtful that a first-century Greek speaker would have understood it that way, for the term always implies a relationship of submission *to an authority*. It is used elsewhere in the New Testament of the submission of Jesus to the authority of his parents (Luke 2:51); of demons being subject to the disciples (Luke 10:17—clearly the meaning "be considerate; act in love" cannot fit here); of citizens being subject to government authorities (Rom. 13:1, 5; Titus 3:1; 1 Pet. 2:13); of the universe being subject to Christ (1 Cor. 15:27; Eph. 1:22); of unseen spiritual powers being subject to Christ (1 Pet. 3:22); of Christ being subject to God the Father (1 Cor. 15:28); of church members being subject to church leaders (1 Cor. 16:15–16 [with 1 Clement 42:4]; 1 Pet. 5:5); of wives being subject to their husbands (Col. 3:18; Titus 2:5; 1 Pet. 3:5; cf. Eph. 5:22, 24); of the church being subject to Christ (Eph. 5:24); of servants being subject to their masters (Titus 2:9; 1 Pet. 2:18); and of Christians being subject to God (Heb. 12:9; James 4:7). None of these relationships is ever reversed; that is, husbands are never told to be subject (*hypotasso*) to wives, the government to citizens, masters to servants, the disciples to demons, etc. (In fact, the term is used outside the New Testament to describe the submission and obedience of soldiers in an army to those of superior rank; see Josephus, *Jewish War* 2.566, 578; 5.309. Cf. the adverb in 1 Clement 37:2 and Henry George Liddell and Robert Scott, *A Greek-English Lexicon*, rev. Henry Stuart Jones and Roderick McKenzie, suppl. E. A. Barber, et al. [Oxford: Clarendon, 1968], 1897, which defines *hypotasso* [passive] to mean "be obedient.") The word is never "mutual" in its force; it is *always one-directional* with reference to submission to an authority. So we may ask, why should we assign a meaning to *hypotasso* in Eph. 5:21 that it never carries anywhere else?

Therefore, it seems to be a misunderstanding of Eph. 5:21 to say that it implies mutual submission. Even in Eph. 5:22–24, wives are to be subject not to everyone or to all husbands but to their "own husbands"—the "submission" Paul has in mind is not a general thoughtfulness toward others but a specific submission to a higher authority. But should not the verb *hypotasso* in v. 22 (whether implicitly or explicitly) take the same sense it does in v. 21?

The mutual submission interpretation is so common because interpreters *assume* that the Greek pronoun *allelous* ("one another") must be completely reciprocal—that is, that it must mean "everyone to everyone." There are several texts where *allelous* does mean "everyone to everyone," but that is not the case in all of its uses, and it certainly does not have to take that meaning. Rather, it often means "some to others." For example, in Rev. 6:4, "so that people should *slay one another*" means "so that *some* would kill *others*" (not "so that every person would kill every other person," or "so that those people being killed would mutually kill those who were killing them," which would make no sense); in Gal. 6:2, "Bear *one another's* burdens" means not "everyone should exchange burdens with everyone else" but "*some* who are more able should help bear the burdens of *others* who are less able"; and in 1 Cor. 11:33, "when you come together to eat, wait for *one another*" means "*some* who are ready early should wait for *others* who are late" (cf. Luke 2:15; 12:1; 24:32—there are many examples where the word is not exhaustively reciprocal). Similarly, in Eph. 5:21, both the following context and the meaning of *hypotasso* require *allelous* here to mean "some to others," so that the verse could be paraphrased, "those who are under authority should be subject to others among you who have authority over them."

Therefore, according to this (second) interpretation, it would seem best to say that in Eph. 5:21 Paul is commanding not "mutual submission" but submission to appropriate authorities.

5. Wayne Grudem, *Evangelical Feminism and Biblical Truth*, 544–99.
6. See the research cited in the previous note.
7. One of the most pertinent Greek witnesses for the meaning "head" in Paul's time comes from Philo of Alexandria, who describes an image of the head on the body as having a role of leadership: "Just as nature conferred the sovereignty [*hegemonian*] of the body on the head when she granted it also possession of the citadel as the most suitable for its kingly rank, conducted it thitherto take command and establish it on high with the whole framework from neck to foot set below it, like the pedestal under the statue, so too she has given the lordship [*to kratos*] of the senses to the eyes." *Special Laws* 3.184.
8. Mary Stewart Van Leeuwen, *Gender and Grace: Love, Work, and Parenting in a Changing World* (Downers Grove, IL: InterVarsity Press, 1990), 238.
9. When we first wrote this essay for *Recovering Biblical Manhood and Womanhood*, the English work most cited on this question was the dissertation

by J. E. Crouch, *The Origin and Intention of the Colossian Haustafel*, Forschungen zur Religion und Literatur des Alten und Neuen Testaments 109 (Göttingen: Vandenhoeck und Ruprecht, 1972). The examples of ostensible parallels translated into English can be read in this work. For more recent research in English on this topic, see James P. Hering, *The Colossian and Ephesian Haustafeln in Theological Context: An Analysis of Their Origins, Relationship, and Message*, American University Studies, ser. 7, Theology and Religion 260 (New York: P. Lang, 2007); M. Y. McDonald, "Reading the New Testament Household Codes in Light of New Research on Children and Childhood in the Roman World," *Studies in Religion* 41, no. 3 (2012): 376–87.

10. The Greek word *prostatis* does not mean "leader" but "helper" or "patron." In the Bible it occurs only here.
11. Some contributors to *Recovering Biblical Manhood and Womanhood* do not endorse this view of New Testament prophecy. They would say that the New Testament gift of prophecy does not continue today because it was part of that uniquely revelatory moment in history and consisted of words having the infallible authority of God. They would say that women could prophesy in this sense but not teach because authority attached so distinctly to the words, not to the person or exposition as it does in teaching.
12. This understanding of prophecy in the New Testament is developed and defended in Wayne Grudem, *The Gift of Prophecy in the New Testament and Today* (Wheaton, IL: Crossway, 1988); Graham Houston, *Prophecy: A Gift for Today?* (Downers Grove, IL: InterVarsity Press, 1989); D. A. Carson, *Showing the Spirit: A Theological Exposition of 1 Corinthians 12–14* (Grand Rapids, MI: Baker, 1987). This view of New Testament prophecy is the one held by the authors of this book, but some contributors to *Recovering Biblical Manhood and Womanhood* hold a different view.
13. See notes 11 and 12.
14. See also Wayne Grudem, "Prophecy, Yes, but Teaching, No: Paul's Consistent Affirmation of Women's Participation without Governing Authority," *Journal of the Evangelical Theological Society* 30, no. 1 (March 1987): 11–23.
15. Ruth Tucker, *Guardians of the Great Commission: The Story of Women in Modern Missions* (Grand Rapids, MI: Zondervan, 1988).
16. Ibid., 38.
17. Ibid., 47.
18. Ibid., 83.
19. A. J. Gordon, "The Ministry of Women," *Gordon-Conwell Monograph* 61 (South Hamilton, MA: Gordon-Conwell Theological Seminary, n.d.), 10. Originally published in *Missionary Review of the World*, n.s., 8, no. 12 (December 1894): 910–21.

20. Dr. and Mrs. Howard Taylor, *Hudson Taylor and the China Inland Mission: The Growth of a Work of God* (London: The Religious Tract Society, 1940), 397–98.
21. Tucker, *Guardians of the Great Commission*, 117.
22. John White, *When the Spirit Comes with Power: Signs and Wonders among God's People* (Downers Grove, IL: InterVarsity Press, 1988), 128.
23. Thesaurus Linguae Graecae (Irvine: University of California at Irvine, 1987), Pilot CD-ROM #C.
24. *Plutarch's Lives of Illustrious Men*, trans. John Dryden (New York: John Wurtele Lovell, n.d.), 3:359.
25. *Index discipulorum* 125.19–20.
26. John Chrysostom, *Homilies on the Epistle of St. Paul the Apostle to the Romans* 31.7, in *A Select Library of the Nicene and Post-Nicene Fathers of the Christian Church*, ed. Philip Schaff, first ser., vol. 11 (Grand Rapids, MI: Eerdmans, 1956), 555.
27. We are perplexed about the fact that in the near context of the citation of Junia, Epiphanius also designates Prisca, who is mentioned in Rom. 16:3, as a man, even though we know from the New Testament that she was a woman.
28. Origen, *Commentaria in Epistolam B. Pauli ad Romanos*, in *Origenis: Opera Omnia*, vol. 14 of *Patrologia Graeca*, ed. J. P. Migne, col. 1289. This work was preserved in a Latin translation by Rufinus (ca. AD 345–ca. 410).
29. A. T. Robertson, *A Grammar of the Greek New Testament in the Light of Historical Research* (New York: Hodder and Stoughton, 1914), 171–73.
30. However, Junia is a common woman's name in Latin, and that has persuaded several recent translations to render the name as Junia.
31. The construction in Greek uses the adjective *episēmos* ("well known") with the expression for "the apostles" in the dative case. Through extensive research in extrabiblical Greek writings, Michael Burer has shown that this construction almost always means "well known to" (when persons are named in the dative case), whereas to say that someone was "well known among" a group (as belonging to the group), Greek writers regularly used the genitive case. See Michael Burer, "'Επίσημοι ἐν τοῖς ἀποστόλοις in Rom 16:7 as 'Well Known to the Apostles': Further Defense and New Evidence," *JETS* 58, no. 4 (2015): 731–55.
32. N. G. L. Hammond and H. H. Scullard, eds., *Oxford Classical Dictionary*, 2nd ed. (Oxford: Clarendon, 1970), 1139.
33. Gerald Sheppard, "A Response to Ray Anderson," *TSF Bulletin* 9, no. 4 (March–April 1986): 21.
34. Karen J. Torjesen, "Sexuality, Hierarchy and Evangelicalism," *TSF Bulletin* 10, no. 4 (March–April 1987): 26–27.
35. "Gay Rights Resolution Divides Membership of Evangelical Woman's Caucus," *Christianity Today* (October 3, 1986): 40–43.

36. Paul Jewett, *Man as Male and Female: A Study in Sexual Relationships from a Theological Point of View* (Grand Rapids, MI: Eerdmans, 1975), 178.
37. Paul Jewett, "An Overlooked Study: John Boswell on Homosexuality," *Reformed Journal* 33, no. 1 (January 1983): 17.
38. Robin Scroggs, *The New Testament and Homosexuality: Contextual Backgrounds for Contemporary Debate* (Philadelphia: Fortress, 1983), 129.
39. Paul Jewett, review of *The New Testament and Homosexuality: Contextual Backgrounds for Contemporary Debate*, by Robin Scroggs, *Interpretation* 39, no. 2 (April 1985): 210.
40. For Jim Wallis, see Leigh Jones, "Jim Wallis Announces Support for Same-Sex Marriage," *World*, April 8, 2013, http://www.worldmag.com/2013/04/jim_wallis_announces_support_for_same_sex_marriage. For Tony Campolo and David Neff, see Warren Cole Smith, "Jockeying for Position on Same-Sex Marriage," *World*, June 10, 2015, http://www.worldmag.com/2015/06/jockeying_for_position_on_same_sex_marriage.
41. Nicholas Wolterstorff, "Hearing the Cry," in *Women, Authority, and the Bible*, ed. Alvera Mickelsen (Downers Grove, IL: InterVarsity Press, 1986), 289.
42. Thomas B. Stoddard, "Gay Adults Should Not Be Denied the Benefits of Marriage," *Minneapolis Star-Tribune*, March 7, 1989, 11A.
43. Emil Brunner, *Das Gebot und die Ordnungen: Entwurf einer protestantisch-theologischen ethik* (Tübingen: J. C. B. Mohr/Paul Siebeck, 1933), 358.
44. Otto Piper, *Christian Ethics* (London: Thomas Nelson and Sons, 1970), 299.
45. See chapter 1 in *Recovering Biblical Manhood and Womanhood*, 44–45, 50–52.
46. Elisabeth Elliot, "Virginity," *Elisabeth Elliot Newsletter*, March/April 1990, 2–3.
47. These quotes are from the *Danvers Statement* of the Council on Biblical Manhood and Womanhood. See appendix.
48. Gretchen Gaebelein Hull, *Equal to Serve: Men and Women in the Church and Home* (Old Tappan, NJ: Fleming H. Revell, 1987), 188–89.

Scripture Index

desiringGod

Everyone wants to be happy. Our website was born and built for happiness. We want people everywhere to understand and embrace the truth that *God is most glorified in us when we are most satisfied in him*. We've collected more than thirty years of John Piper's speaking and writing, including translations into more than forty languages. We also provide a daily stream of new written, audio, and video resources to help you find truth, purpose, and satisfaction that never end. And it's all available free of charge, thanks to the generosity of people who've been blessed by the ministry.

If you want more resources for true happiness, or if you want to learn more about our work at Desiring God, we invite you to visit us at www.desiringGod.org.

www.desiringGod.org

Additional Resources on Biblical Manhood and Womanhood

For more information, visit crossway.org.